Essay Index

FOOL'S ADVICE

FOOL'S ADVICE

BY
EDGAR A. SINGER, Jr.

Essay Index Reprint Series

Originally Published by
HENRY HOLT AND COMPANY
NEW YORK

BOOKS FOR LIBRARIES PRESS
FREEPORT, NEW YORK

Essay Index

INTERNATIONAL STANDARD BOOK NUMBER:
0-8369-2442-8

LIBRARY OF CONGRESS CATALOG CARD NUMBER:
78-167420

PRINTED IN THE UNITED STATES OF AMERICA
BY
NEW WORLD BOOK MANUFACTURING CO., INC.
HALLANDALE, FLORIDA 33009

FOREWORD

To "Old Students of Mine."

There is little in the past our philosophy
goes regretting; but if one thing more than
others, it is the *leisure of the Garden*. One
says "Garden" out of habit, for the beauty
of the image; Street or Porch it might have
been, or just Academy—the thing is not the
landscape, but those quiet stately figures
walking, talking *at their leisure*.

Conversing—that is it, discussing with each
other. Their leisure was not idle, but argument unhurried. And what argument there
was "about it and about"!—the best of our
science we owe to that debate.

Well, things are changed, and not all for
the better. Hundreds of silent eyes greet
the "master" of this day, as stepping on his
platform he unfolds his lecture; then, of
tongues not a one. It would be indecent;
a Course must be rounded; let the artist have
his way! The students of our colleges are

v

hopelessly polite to Professors always busy, always busy. . . .

Let me tell you, O Old Students, it's no fun to be so busy. And that is why, when from time to time you have asked for a "talk on what you will," I have willed it to be idle, and chat of idle things. You seemed not to mind it, but laughed with or at me— I care not which. These were *your* occasions; we were fellow-students, playfellows if you please. "Leisure" there was for once to round out nothing, to say things somewhat doubtful, to try untrodden ways. For time was there for "come-backs," once more we could debate it as in the ancient days when thought experimented—*tried-on* ideas.

Of the wisdom of these occasions, some fragments are before you, all properly entitled *Fool's Advice*. "And in bringing them together (you are free to grumble) 'tis such advice he followed." *Let* it be. But the years the locust which eateth all our years hath eaten—perchance these fragments may restore them to you. They brought them back to me.

University of Pennsylvania,
1925.   E. A. S.

CONTENTS

THE MONASTICISM OF MR. KNOX

To the Graduate Club

THE MONASTICISM OF MR. KNOX

What recommends Mr. Knox to the heart and conscience of the philosopher is his solicitude for method. He thinks it no waste, and of course it is none, to begin a short paper on matters of life and death with a long analysis of the ways life and death—or it might be dinner and supper, trapezoids and Zoroastrianism—are to be met with. You may come on any of them from the historical, from the geographical, or from the logical point of view. "Thus if your subject be cannibalism, you may trace the history of cannibalism throughout the centuries; show in what state of society it arose, what circumstances tended to enhance its popularity, how it has flourished at times in impure forms, and in a half-hearted sort of way; you may suggest some of the causes which contributed to its gradual decline, and estimate the value, not to be lightly underrated, of the permanent effect which it has left, as a stage in

3

the development of civilization, adding, of course, that all which was best in it has been taken up into the common store of our national institutions, and will remain forever as part of the inalienable heritage of the race. Or you may take it geographically, indicating the parts of the world in which it has appeared, speculating as to whether it arose independently in each, or was handed on from one place to another in the course of a gradual interpenetration and diffusion of thought, remarking on the various modifications in its practices to which national or climatic conditions have given rise, and concluding in a general way, that whereas it would clearly be wrong for us, we are by no means at liberty to reprehend in others the observance of customs which have won so wide an acceptance and endeared themselves so deeply to the unspoilt mind of the savage. Or you may take it from the logical point of view, and show that, after all, cannibalism is not the same thing as head-hunting, nor yet the same thing as eating beef, nor yet the same thing as cremation; you may discuss whether its origin was practical, due to a

shortage of food; or ritual, due to a belief
in the possibility of absorbing moral qualities by physical assimilation; or hygienic, being merely a primitive form of the modern
food-fad; and you may point out that what
has been done at all sorts of times, and all
over the place, is not necessarily right, or
healthy, or gentlemanly, and that we are
bound to find some permanent and valuable
underlying principle in it before we recom-
mend it to adoption in our own age and circumstances. And that I conceive to be the
most illuminating and the most sensible way
of going to work, and furthermore the most
easy because it does not involve frequent ref-
erence to, and even quotation from, standard
works on the subject, such as Schink's 'Out-
growth of Mansfleshculture in the Primitive
Folksepochs' on the one hand, or Fothergill's
'Fifteen Years in a Fijian Larder' on the
other."

Who shall say that waste is wasted when
such a bare exposition of method can lift a
reader out of his worries and embarrass-
ments? I wanted very much to lay before
you the central thought of this paper, though

perhaps you wonder why I should. However fitting and proper a subject for Mr. Knox to discuss before the Oxford society De Rebus Ecclesiasticis, you will want to know what monasticism, especially when it is to be discussed neither from the geographical nor from the historical point of view, can have to do with you. "We were not aware," you will be modestly saying to yourselves, "that we had acquired any special reputation for devoutness." That may be so, but are you not graduate students? And am I not right in supposing that graduate studies lead (D. V.) to the academic life? And do we not have it on the very best of authority (the authority of the man of affairs himself) that the academic is a cloistered soul? How then, since you have asked me to address you, should I miss an opportunity to lay before you the very latest opinion as to what the life of the cloister is and means?

Hence my topic, Monasticism. But if monasticism, then surely Mr. Knox, for nowhere else, I venture to say, will you find an analysis of monasticism so intelligible to every kind of monk, whether actual like me or potential like you, as in the article from which I am quoting. You would quite expect this, even if you had somehow managed to miss last February's number of the "English Church Review," were you acquainted with Mr. Knox. But I dare say you are not, for though there are a thousand reasons why you might well like to be, there is just one why it would be wonderful if you were. That one is Mr. Knox's passion for privacy. His first two works (so far as I have been able to find out, they are his first) were privately and even anonymously printed under the titles, "Absolute And Abitofhell," and "Reunion All Around." The article before me I take to be his third writing. It is indeed acknowledged to be the work of the Rev. Ronald A. Knox, but then entrusted to the aforementioned "Church Review," where I suppose its author thought himself reasonably safe from intrusion. The case is somewhat different with the fourth and last writing that has come to my notice: it is quite brazenly set forth to be the contribution of Mr. Knox, "Chaplain Fellow of Trinity College, Oxford." It is a small tract for the use

of soldiers in the trenches. I am not in-
formed, but I rather think that if one were
in a hurry to find Mr. Knox just at this
moment [1915], there are more likely places
in which to look for him than in his rooms
at Trinity.

But I was saying when interrupted by
these questions,—Why Monasticism? and,
Who's Knox?—I was saying that Mr.
Knox's scrupulous definition of method at
the very outset of his paper had served me
mightily. We are to take the point of view
of logic, says he. Yet fortunate as this is
for me, I doubt if I should have been clever
enough to find it out for myself from the
mere reading of what follows. Not that I
should have called the procedure geographical nor yet historical exactly, but perhaps I
should have imagined a fourth method,
which had it been the real one would have
baffled me completely. I think I should have
called it the way of the finished artist, and
from the work of the artist one can leave
nothing out; one can't even change the order
of it. How happy I was then to recall that
the master of the feast had ordered and ar-

ranged it in so tempting a way only of his courtesy and urbanity, but that his ultimate purpose in inviting a fellow to it was not the delighting but the nourishing of his soul. Thus am I relieved and justified if after the manner of a logician, of whom one expects no grace and no art save that of simplification, I spoil all the beauty of a pleasant thing by reducing it to an affair of axioms and theorems.

Now Mr. Knox has two axioms, I think, but at any rate he has one. It is this, *Monasticism is waste.* "It is at this point that the real quarrel the modern world has with monasticism is bound to arise. The modern world cannot appreciate the absolute value of waste. The spirit in which widows immolated themselves on their husbands' pyres; the spirit in which a man was ready to risk his life in order to avenge a fancied slight put upon him by an acquaintance, that spirit has, for us, nothing admirable. It flickered again for a moment even in the nineteenth century, when Dante Gabriel Rossetti threw his unpublished poems into his wife's open grave; its death-warrant was sealed when he took them out again to publish them, some years later. Now, I am not defending either Suttee or duelling; I disapprove of both. But I disapprove of them, not because of the spirit of wastefulness which inspired them; I disapprove of them because they turned that spirit to an entirely wrong account. The one involved self-murder, the other a risk of murdering other people; the one assumes that a man is master of his own wife, the other that a man is keeper of his own dignity, both very pestilent points of view. But I do still think there is something to be said for the spirit of waste."

Whatever is ultimately to be said for the spirit of waste, the divinely simple and efficient mechanism of logic gives us at once a theorem out of our axiom: If monasticism is waste, then what involves no waste cannot be monastic. There are false ideas on the subject. Take first this "picture of two strangely dissimilar things—the average Englishman's idea of a monk and the average Englishman's idea of a nun. A monk is a very fat, very hearty old soul, in a brown habit with a dressing-gown cord; he spends his time between a chapel, where he takes snuff and sleeps through the recitation of the Divine Office, and the Refectory, where he consumes an abnormal quantity of turkey, plum-pudding, and liqueurs. He goes out hunting every day in the week, except Thursdays, when he sits waiting for the inevitable Friday fish at the inevitable monastic fishpond. His chief reason for fleeing from the world is that in the world you have to make your own living instead of exacting it from your tenants.

"The nun is a far more interesting and etherealized creature. She was crossed in love, an early attachment blighted, and fell back upon the cloister with the natural tendency of a soul in distress. She wanders about most of the time in a large and obtrusively walled garden, and does a good deal of pining among the lilies. She is invariably pale, thin, and consumptive. Her sole employment is a series of ecstasies, in the course of which she receives divine revelations, to be recorded on paper for the consolation of the world which has treated her so hardly. Wasted? No, not wasted, for her life, it is assumed, would have been spent in the Bath-chair if it had not been spent on a Miserere. If she has got to pine away, she might as well do it in a convent; whereas the monk, if he must put on flesh, might at least have had the decency to do it outside of a monas-tery. . . .

"In a word, the whole mainspring of a monastic life must be renunciation, and re-nunciation is at best only partial and second-best, unless the life you are spurning and leaving behind is one that might have been full and fruitful elsewhere. If you are to renounce the world, you must have a world to renounce. It is possible (we must discuss later in what sense) that the vocation to a religious life demands a specialized set of faculties, not possessed, even potentially, by every one who is born into the world. But this must not be taken to imply that those flowers could not have blossomed anyhow in any other soil. It may be true that Queen Elizabeth could not have been a first-rate nun. But nobody will ever persuade me that St. Catherine of Siena could not have been a first-rate empress."

I have not wished to venture an opinion as yet on what may be said for the spirit of waste, but I must insist with all the authority of a professional logician on the rigor of this inference: If monasticism is waste, then one who has nothing to waste cannot be a cloistered soul. And there is a second misunderstanding brought to light by our theorem, No waste, no cloister. It has sometimes been thought that if monasticism was to be defended at all, it must be because it was good for something. But then, if monasticism is waste, and if what is not waste is not monasticism, and if what is good for something is not wasted, it follows . . . In short, if monasticism is to be defended it cannot be defended from the point of view of efficiency. Take Fra Angelico, now! "When Fra Angelico painted on his knees, did he do it because he found he painted better on his knees? Or because he found it more comfortable painting on his knees? Of course, it may have been something of both, but I feel very confident that if some one had come up and pointed out to him that his work was actually suffering from the conditions in which it was produced, he would have continued to paint on his knees. The modern world's argument may take either of two forms—it may either say, 'It is your duty to realize yourself and all that is in you to the fullest possible extent,' or it may say, 'The important thing is not to go to work in this or that way, but at all costs to produce your best, as a legacy from your life to the world's treasury.' But if somebody had said to Fra Angelico, 'By remaining on your knees you are wasting your talent of producing superlatively good pictures,' he would have replied, 'Yes, but by painting superlatively good pictures I should waste my talent for remaining on my knees.' And the other argument he would not have recognized at all."

With this picture of waste uncompromising the logician would gladly end his account of asceticism; then his saint might go off the stage in a round halo of consistency. And for the matter of that we might well enough stop here if we were dealing with the asceticism of the East or of Schopenhauer. For such asceticism life is so bad that it is best

to waste it as wastefully as we know how.
But we are not of the East and we are not
with Schopenhauer; we are with Mr. Knox,
an Englishman and rather one of us, who like
the rest of us would rather let logic go hang
than let waste be altogether wasted. There
are certain phrases: One wastes to acquire
merit; One wastes ad majorem Dei gloriam.
These ancient phrases, sweet with the odor of
incense, musical with a rumor of golden
crowns cast down 'round glassy seas, do they
mean something or do they not? Here is
our difficulty and our quandary. If these
phrases are but phrases, memories, umbræ
idearum, then our asceticism is Eastern,
Schopenhauerian, a thing of disappointments
and despairs; only our logic is saved; waste
is all wasted and life less welcome than death.
But if to acquire merit is to acquire something of worth and of passing worth, if
God's glory is something to be valued above
all other values, then whatever renunciation
is needed to acquire merit and to magnify
God is not wasted. He does not waste opportunity who turns down his glass of an evening that he may dance to the morning's sun.

Our hearts are light; only our logic suffers, for waste is not wasted.

Now I have no doubt in my own mind which of these two varieties of waste Mr. Knox takes monasticism to be. And I have no more doubt that if any one ventured to remind him that he had said something at the outset about a determination to be logical, he would reply that the use of logic wasn't so much to avoid contradictions as to make them explicit. I have no doubt at all that he would gaily accept as his second axiom the proposition, *Waste is not wasted.* He could still pen without sense of inconsistency his last sentence and final estimate of monasticism, "Monasticism preaches that spirit of Christian routine, which is valuable just as all routine is valuable, because you cannot take credit for it; valuable, because when you have done it for a lifetime, you not only call yourself, but feel yourself, an unprofitable servant."

I mean in short that if Mr. Knox were here he could defend himself better than I can defend him, but isn't that an ill-conditioned and unmannered soul who puts on the absent the burden of maintaining a contradiction he himself accepts and only wishes he might have had the wit to invent?   But these two axioms are indeed the expression of all I have found academic life to be when it is lived at its highest and its best.   It is a life of waste and Verschwenden; while through it runs the baffling, torturing, inspiring thought: Surely somehow, somewhere, somewhen this waste is not wasted.   Wherefore I regretfully part company with Mr. Knox at this point to take up the story for myself, to attempt to show in my own poor way how our life is waste and how its waste is not wasted.

Of course I know there are many of my colleagues who would say that I am giving myself unnecessary trouble, who would deny the waste and object to, even resent, the likening of themselves to cloistered souls. And it would be useless to deny that just as there are monks with no vocation for monasticism, so there are academics who waste not. A few there may be, a very few I think, who like Mr. Knox's fat monk and phthisic nun waste nothing because they have nothing to waste. These will be those who inspired Mr. Bernard Shaw to observe that "Those who can, do; those who can't, teach." But it is not at all to this class that belongs the more vehement academic soul who refuses to be put along with the cloistered. He will be thinking rather of the great services a university performs for the State, not only in training its citizens in good citizenship, but also and even chiefly in placing highly expert knowledge at the disposal of the community. And he will point out in passing that the college professor is no recluse, but comes in contact with the widest possible humanity; that if he does spend a portion (and not the least pleasant portion) of his time in the society of immature minds, he would very soon cease to be of any use or interest to this immaturity were he to spend too much of his time in its company. Finally, my protestant against the cloister may take it upon him to show that college professors have made excellent ambassadors, governors, presidents, and what not.

But when all this has been admitted, what

does it show? Only that there are academics
who have plenty to waste and who are glad
to give for the fun of giving what of their
efficiency they are not obliged to market for
the sake of living. What does not appear is
that the contemplation of his efficiencies,
whether important or not, has anything to do
with the deeper motives of the academic's
life. His utility may keep him going; it
cannot keep him living. Over against this
college professor who is training citizens, I
put the lonely figure of an Amiel; over
against that other who is investigating cor-
porations, I put the image of a Gauss, quietly
thanking God that no one had yet found use
for his sort of mathematics. Ah, yes, no
doubt Catherine of Siena could have made a
first-rate empress, but then she would not, or
only as the last, the greatest and the hardest
of her renunciations.

I know, however, that it is not the academic
most impressed with the sense of his utility
who reacts most violently against the appel-
lation of cloistered soul. It is rather just
the waster and dreamer of dreams. Perhaps
yourselves will have experienced something

of this feeling of shocked amazement, when first the voice of affairs explained your affair to you. Very likely you had just realighted on your golden bough, your wings still trembling with the effort of your flight, when first there came to your ear the refrain of the chorus. Doubting your senses, you may have cocked a wondering eye at the placid pool from which this music came, and you may have said to yourself, "If that isn't the same old grandfather of finance basking on the same old stone; if those eyes are not the same bulging eyes of coming captains of industry protruding from the waters; if those are not the same small fry of affairs busily pullulating beneath, seeing to it that the bottom does not drop out of things—why then at any rate the scene and all the actors are indistinguishably like those I left behind me when last I spread my wings." Meanwhile, where have you not been; what things have you not seen; what recondite harmonies have you not divined up there among the spheres? You, the shut-in soul! You, the cloistered intelligence! "Breckeckeckex yourself," you say, "I am beginning to feel my bottom getting very sore, my dear little Koax-koax."

But, my Dionysian, you will permit an old fellow to hope that if you were ever tempted to answer the chorus in this spirit, you will by this time have outgrown your impatience. For in the first place it is unmannerly to address in this way the beloved of the Muses, of the goat-footed Pan, the delight of Apollo, god of the lyre, those who make to grow in the marshes the very rushes from which your lyre is built. And in the second place their ancient wisdom is right; your flighty Dionysian spirit is even the cloistered thing they say it is. For there are two kinds of cloister; there is the cloister that shuts in, and there is the cloister that leaves out.

Perhaps you will let me make my meaning clearer by telling an erudite story. There was once a commentator much perplexed by the legend which Diogenes Laertius has set down, of how Hippasos lost his life for revealing the mystic teaching of the Pythagoreans. What troubled the scrupulous spirit of this commentator was to imagine what secrets the Pythagoreans could have had to conceal. He reflected that the most important doctrines concerning life and death associated with the name of Pythagoras, were known to the general public in Pythagoras' own day; he considered further that from what we know of the rules and regulations of the order, their matters of monastic discipline were too trivial to be worth concealing. But after patient consideration he found a solution to his difficulties that sounds plausible enough. He recalled the Pythagoreans to have been, among other things, interested in mathematics; he considered how likely it was that at least this part of their science should have kept itself secret, as it has for the most part managed to do down to the present day. For throughout the centuries the world has been pouring its gold into the pockets of the mathematicians in the hope of seducing them into a betrayal of their mystery. The mathematicians, accepting the bribe, have appeared to labor and to sweat at the imparting of their lore; but for most of the world their secret remains as much their secret as it ever was, and seems likely to remain so forever. Am I not justified in calling the mathematician a cloistered soul? It is not that any walls shut him in: it is that his lofty science leaves most of us out.

I think I am not mistaken in saying that the academic life knows all there is to be known of melancholy, and that no one can teach the thinker what discouragement means. All this is natural product of his waste, which, just in proportion as it is whole-hearted, leaves him poor and lonely. I have sometimes tried to explain to myself, and I will try to explain to you, what such a life has to offer in return for all its Ver-schwenden, why in spite of its black days it is more sunlit than other lives. Not that it makes much difference whether my guess is right or wrong, so far as this might affect your choice or any man's. If it were deadly and all black, one who cared for this life would sell his soul to have it, and I hope I am addressing none who are not ready to sell their souls to get what they want, espe-cially when what they want is the unattain-able. No, the thing is merely intellectual and amusing; I would not change the think-er's life for any other; if it were all hell, it would still be my own preference in the way of a hell, and I should like it better than somebody else's heaven.

Now, if I meant to persuade—but I have no more gift for persuasion than for dissuasion—yet if I did want to be encouraging, I might stop to point out that to understand loneliness is to have gotten to the very core of the universal heart. It is true, so far as I can make out, that by busying yourselves with the affairs of the æther, you may come to understand a cutthroat or a pickpocket rather better than can the chap who gets up statistics or runs a mission in the slums. I mean that thugs and thinkers differ only in their manner of achieving loneliness; the world that has cast out the one has been cast off by the other, but however they have come to be alone, they ought to understand each other.

But I am not concerned with mere palliatives, and if I were, I am not sure that a peculiar insight into the ways of sin would seem to every saint pay for his saintliness. There are those who would rather hear of truth, of new-minted truth, than of world-

old sin and naughtiness. Yet forgive me
if I wonder whether there is as much joy
in the finding of new truth as has sometimes been said. If the interpretation of
history were left to me, I should say that
new truth was as painful as new boots; new
truth is so unpleasant a thing that it has
created a prejudice against all truth. For we
only speak of *truth* when it is new. Old
and well broken-in to our needs, we ask it no
questions and call it no names. This prejudice against truth is a mistake, of course.
Truth is neither beautiful nor ugly; but
when it is new we are not adjusted to it, and
so it hurts—sometimes most abominably.
However, if the discovery of new truth is no
tragedy, neither is it comic and lightsome;
to enter on the monastic life for the sake of
so equivocal a heaven is not to have counted
the cost. Well, then what? There are those
who speak confidently of contributing to the
development of humanity. But what is that
—the development of humanity? To acquire merit and to glorify God are not
vaguer accounts of the unwaste of our wasted
lives than is this ideal of development.

There is a poet who told of one that
dreamed he had lived through the song of
a bird, but woke to find a hundred years
had passed. And there have been mathematicians who made out the convergence of
an infinite series when they had caught the
law and trend of a few of its terms. And
there is the story of a God to whom it is
said a thousand years are as a day, and a
day as a thousand years. Poet, mathematician, God, are alike in this, that they grasp
eternity in a flash; for them heaven is less
a place than it is a direction, a tangent, a
differential coefficient. Vaguely and most
imperfectly I seem to see that the solace of
your monastic lives must be your *sense of
the north*, as Du Maurier has put it. Not
after a while, but now or never must you
know all there is of heaven. Either the
blessed life is altogether spent in the music
of crowns cast down 'round glassy seas, or
it is useless to wait for the time when these
things shall come to be. Heaven, sirs, is
a direction, not a destiny. I have always
found this direction to be uphill and not a
little precipitous, but one grows to like preci-

pices when one feels oneself to be tumbling up them, rather than falling down.

If then to bring this rambling discourse to a close I were to try to say a last word for the spirit of waste, it would be this: In order that progress should be made, there must be men ready to work alone and to forego not only the ordinary forms of recognition but even that last sustenance of the spirit, confidence in one's self. There must be days when one has to look back on patient labor come to nothing, experiments of no result, sincere efforts at expression expressive only of the grimace of effort. On such days there is no one in all the universe to applaud; one stands desperately alone, and the waste seems all waste and that waste all folly. The man who can live through such days and look forward to more of them without wishing he had accepted as his part in life something a little softer, even if less sound —that man is the true ascetic.

But if I might I would give him this to reflect on. In order that the great experiment of informing matter with the form of thought shall go on, someone must live just such a life as he is living; one who is prepared to stop nowhere in the prodigality of his wasting. This someone is the rare, the ascetic, the heaven-inspired soul who in order that he should feel his waste unwasted must realize that in doing his part to make the infinite series converge he is making for himself right here and now all the blessedness there is for him or any man.

Wherefore my last word to all about to enter the cloister will be this: See ye waste well, that ye be not wasted.

FOOL'S ADVICE

To the Philomathean Society

FOOL'S ADVICE

Your Commencement Orator has many qualities justly endearing him to the public heart, so endearing him that, though for these hundred years he has been known to say nothing worth listening to, yet it is a fair guess hundreds of years to come will invite him annually to repeat it. It is his manner that is irresistible. Not every day do you meet with one so affable, so pleased with everything that has happened, so willing everybody should be pleased with everything happened or likely to happen. He is determinedly cheerful, or if in spite of him a trace of tears seep into his voice as he speaks of partings, the world about understands these tears to be all his own, while benches of young pagans face the prospect with dry-eyed stoicism. Above all things he is hopeful. Not that he is unaware of some little contrarieties life has had in store for those who have tried it before; but hoping

31

is always an inexpensive and therefore reasonable luxury; there is no reason your orator should spare it you.   Thus all Commencement Orators; or if one star differeth from another star in glory, it can only be in the tastefulness and discrimination of a choice in hopings.   May mine commend itself to your judgment, Gentlemen of Philo.

To begin with, I pray your lives may be free from all unrest of inner doubt and harassment of outer caviling.   To which end I would devise it if I could that you be and remain as ordinary, commonplace and humdrum as possible.   Let your thought be of this day its daily bread, with perhaps a prospect, not too eagerly to be dwelt on, of just a little butter for to-morrow.   To the calm eye of the philosopher those who have thus chosen, or to whom the Fates have vouchsafed it so, are indeed the most blessed of men.   It is true, we observe many so blest to complain in their first youth and inexperience of a certain monotony in the prospect, from which they are prone to seek relief in ways we cannot always approve.   They try

doors fondly thought to open on some fourth
dimension—various according to the variety
of their imagination. So this one gets exceeding drunk and is rude to his wife; that
one attends radical meetings and advocates
with too much vehemence new and untried
theories for the world's betterment. But
the eternal harmony and just equipoise of
things is not long upset by these little aber-
rancies. Lo, to the one, Nature, well abetted
by wives abused, brings salutary remorse;
briefly is he back to his bench again, out-
wardly chastened, inwardly refreshed. The
other after none too long a trial of them dis-
covers his fellow laborers in the vineyard
to be wanting no better world, if to be better a world must be different. But the first
pangs of disillusionment past, our revolu-
tionist learns resignation, continuing therein
until those once wayward feet find rest at
last under a generous spread of bank-presi-
dential mahogany.

All this I would choose for you; and will
you not say I have chosen wisely and well?
But alas! even as I utter them a misgiving
takes me these hopes for you are well-nigh

hopeless. In voicing them, I remind myself
of nothing more than of that good parson who
consented to pray for rain; "though I fear,"
said he, "it will naught avail with the wind
in this quarter." That is it, you see, the
wind is in the wrong quarter to blow you to
the blessed isles I would have destined you
to. Or rather, do not blame the wind! It
is you who have, with culpable disregard of
sound advice, steered out of the course.
What perversity induced men of your original intelligence to follow the ways of
schools and colleges, when any of your elders could have shown you these ways to
be futile ways where indeed they were not
evil ones? Their routine learning stupefies
genius, their care for things gone discourages
self-expression, their brooding on old thought
spoils young life of its zest. On this all history is so of one mind as to leave no doubt
but things have gone from bad to worse always. For what your elders would have
pointed out to you, their elders had pointed
out to them, Rousseau to their elders, Montaigne to Rousseau, Rabelais to Montaigne,
while as early as Plato's time it was plain

schools had done nothing but run downhill for generations. I judge then the iniquities of schools, if not very honorable, to be at least very ancient; and as the knowledge of this seems assimilable only by those too old to profit by it, the harm done by centuries of going to school must by this time have grown beyond calculation. It is now generally admitted by your elders that all a man gains from a liberal education is an ability to read in the original the excellent reasons there are for not indulging in liberal education.

Clearly then, the very occasion gathering you together to hear my hopes for you is evidence enough I may not hope too much of you. You have let yourselves be corrupted. From the very beginning of your residence within these walls you have been beset with temptations to think. At rare intervals and timidly at first, then with ever-increasing boldness, those who are set here to be your guides have stopped your ready answers to ask, "How do you know?" "What do you mean?" In short, with the cunning of their craft, they have sought to

seduce you into their own vice, the proper
ugly name of which is *Reason*. I dare say
you put up a brave fight against this seduc-
tion at first. In fact I am sure of it, and
shall always be ready to bear testimony to
the obstinate valor of most. But have all
withstood to the end? Have not some succumbed? Are none sunk from the high
plane of man to the level of rational animals?

Indeed I fear the worst. I fear lest not
one, or a few, but many or most have ceased
to confine their outlook on life to the day
and the morrow, but have let it search into
the far away, let it dwell upon the long run,
let it scrutinize the end. Here at the very
threshold of life they have stopped to be
thoughtful, have considered within themselves what direction they should give to
their lives as a whole.

All this is bad, of course, but not as bad
as it might be, not as bad as it surely will be
if you heed not the counsel of prudence
while yet there is time. Now prudence'
counsel is, to follow the wisdom of the
fathers. But the fathers will tell you there

are fifteen, two hundred and fifty, or there-
about careers, to follow any one of which
is highly honorable—*if* you succeed in it.
So then if think you must, let your thought
be of success, of your fitness, of your opportunity; consulting, without letting yourself
be too much controlled by, any little dictates
of taste or predilection you may discover in
yourself. So begin, and thereafter let not
your thoughts wander from the object that
is your life-object; but living each day not
for its own sake, not for any beauty it may
hold, but for the sake of the whole, strive
on to ultimate success. So do, and the vice
of your schooling will not greatly have
harmed you. You may have missed the perfection of the humdrum, but you will not
have missed it by much, and my best hopes
for you will not all have gone a-glimmering.

Thus far, you perceive, I have been able
to preserve a certain cheerfulness in my outlook for you, under however discouraging
conditions. I have assumed, or feigned to
assume, that however you had lost yourselves
in thought, you would not have let the native
hue of your resolution be all sicklied o'er with

the pale cast of it; that you would let reason be the servant of prudence, accepting as
a prudent man should at the hands of the
past the good purposes of life, confining your
intelligence to the winning of these approved
ends.   Thus may you still travel well-worn
ways.   But now for a while my thoughts
must take a graver turn, my reflections a more
somber tone.   For there are those, there have
always been those, who instead of using their
reason prudently must set themselves to
think out the reason for prudence; instead of
employing their intelligence in the clever
adaptation of means to end, must needs know
whether the ends proposed have anything to
say for themselves that the reason can understand.   And then there is the devil to pay.

I sometimes wonder what Purun Bhagat
thought about as he sat at the mouth of
Kali's shrine, high in the Himalayas, and
gazed down upon the valley.   "He knew"—
we are told—"he knew for a certainty that
there was nothing great and nothing little in
this world; and day and night he strove to
think out his way into the heart of things,

back to the place whence his soul had come."

You remember how he came to be dwelling in Kali's Shrine; how he had once been a great minister of state, honored, famous; how that last time he returned to India from his travels "there was a blaze of glory, for the Viceroy himself made a special visit to confer upon the Maharajah the Grand Cross of the Star of India—all diamonds and ribbons and enamel; and at the same ceremony, while the cannon boomed, Purun Dass was made a Knight Commander of the Order of the Indian Empire; so that his name stood Sir Purun Dass, K.C.I.E. . . .

"Next month, when the city had returned to its sunbaked quiet, he did a thing no Englishman would have dreamed of doing; for so far as the world's affairs went, he died."

He died, but we catch another glimpse of this dead man. He is walking the long, white, dusty Indian road. "At night his antelope skin was spread where the darkness overtook him—sometimes in a Sunnyasi monastery by the roadside; sometimes by a mud-pillar shrine of Kala Pir . . . ; sometimes on

the outskirts of a little Hindu village, where
the children would steal up with the food
their mothers had prepared; and sometimes
on the pitch of the bare grazing grounds,
where the flame of his stick fire waked the
drowsy camels. It was all one to Purun Dass
—or Purun Bhagat, as he called himself now.
Earth, people, and food were all one."

So he fared, and so he came to the Hills,
to the Himalayas. Here, said Purun Bhagat,
shall I find peace. And he found peace, for
"he knew for a certainty that there was
nothing great and nothing little in this world;
and day and night he strove to think out his
way into the heart of things." I wonder
what he found there; I wonder what he
saw. But we know what the wise men of
Purun's race have always said they found
at the heart of things. They have called it
Nirvana, Nothingness, Nothing.

Many, many more than you dream, many
of all centuries and all times have thought
their way into the heart of things and found
there—Nothing. And his biographer is only
partly right when he says of Sir Purun Dass,
K.C.I.E., that "he did a thing no English-

man would have dreamed of doing when, so
far as the world's affairs went, he died."
There are to-day all around you Purun
Dasses who, so far as the world's affairs go,
are dead. Of course, they do not wear a
Sunnyasi's garb, nor sport a begging bowl.
They still turn up at the office of a morning
and dress for dinner of an evening. And as
for begging bowls, neither our private nor
our public conscience is adjusted to them.
We rather make a point of it to gain a living
while we appear to live, and in dying to put
on such unmistakable symptoms of death as
will relieve the living of farther care for us.
But for all that there are men about you
who have looked into the heart of things,
seen it to be empty and abided by this insight. As they retain the outer appearance
of other men you would not know them for
what they are, unless you knew them very
well—and perhaps not then. Sometimes
there are little signs by which the wise might
guess. They like to be with children much
and children much with them, as Purun
Bhagat would gather birds and beasts about
him. They are likely to be exceeding gentle;

they do not seem sad.   In all else they are
as we are.

Now I suppose no man could wish for
another that his thought should end in such
an insight as this; not even one whose own
thought had so ended.   As lief would he
disturb the dreams of a sleeping child.   But
this I beg of you, if ever you should meet
with a Purun Bhagat, do not try to break his
quiet with noise, to move his rest with energy.
My son, will he say to you, the magpies make
an excellent noise, and the gnats seem very
busy.   What think you?   Is it because they
have thought better than I, or because they
have thought not at all?   Ay, there you have
it.   It is thought that has led men to find
Nirvana.   Nothing but more thought can
lead beyond, if indeed there be a beyond.
Is there?   It has been said there is. . . .

With what tender wistfulness has many
a man turned his eyes, tired with science, to
that "Beyond" the olden monks so plainly
saw and lived in faith of.   None more dead
than they "so far as this world's affairs go."
None better than they had thought them-

selves into the heart of things and found
there, so far as this world's affairs go, Nothing. "For all is burdensome to me, whatso-
ever this world offereth for my consolation,"
cries one of them. And he too died, but with
what different vision!

"O most blessed mansion of the city
which is above; O most clear day of eternity,
which night obscureth not! O day ever
joyful, ever secure and never changing! To
the Saints it shineth. . . ."

Who has not closed his *De imitatione* and
wistfully turned his eyes, tired with science,
to where Thomas à Kempis pointed, has indeed not lived all there is to live. And no
doubt many an eye, even a modern eye weary
with science, has found its rest there; but
must it not first or last have lost the keenness
of its scientific vision?

And is there nought, you ask, that science
can see, and philosophy, beyond the mist of
Purun Bhagat, more demonstrable than the
vision of à Kempis? Perhaps nothing, perhaps this. . . . But let me begin by asking
a question.

What is the actual experience of life that

so many thinkers have summed up in that one
word, Nothing?   For it seems to be far from
nothing to live and struggle, to love and
suffer, to face death and die.   But do they
not mean by Nothing, nothing *more;* nothing
better, because nothing *different;* eternal
sameness?   Sameness equals nothingness to
a certain like of soul; and as our thinkers
measured life with a large measure, they
found only repetition, eternal returning.
The East likened it to a revolving wheel.
Of those Puruns of our Western world of
whom I have spoken, one has called it "a
ritournelle". . .

Amiel one day looks back over his diary
of twenty-nine years, the intimate private
by-product of what was to the public just
the usual untroubled, well-behaved college
professor's life.   These thousands of pages
that resume the impressions of a sensitive
soul, can they, he wonders, yield a drop of
essence?   "A forest of cinchonas is worth
but its phial of healing quinine, a whole rose
garden of Smyrna but its drop of attar."
And from these pages—what?

Nothing, perhaps.   "This gossip of the

years sums up perhaps to nothing at all. No
man cares beyond his personal romance and
life. And so . . . And so what?

"Thou wilt have lived, Amiel, and life
consists in repeating the human type; it is
the human ritournelle stepped as it has been
stepped, as it is being stepped, as it will be
stepped for centuries and centuries by le-
gions of thy kind. To know it to be such
a ritournelle is something; it is all we can
do. The realization of the type is sometimes
happier, the ritournelle more joyous, when
circumstances are propitious and clement.
But the marionettes, let them do this, let them
do that—

Trois p'tits tours, et puis s'en vont!

All falls into the same gulf, and comes,
nearly speaking, to nearly the same thing."

There you have it, as I think. If the long
story of this world, as you review it in your
thought, writes but the same page over and
over again, what better can you do than
patiently to wait for your chapter's close?
careful, as an honest gentleman should be,
not to get in the way of your neighbors who

seem to be enjoying the play; reserving your
private reflections for your private journal,
which I think it would be more comely to
burn ere you retire for the night.

Sameness, nothingness; nothingness, sameness! Ah yes, these are the same and are
nothing. But is there no other way of reading this long world-story as it unfolds itself
to our thought? Sometimes I seem to see
there is. Let me close my cheerful discourse by telling as nearly as I can what at
such moments I seem to make out.

Back there, a long way back, I see an ani-
mal that walks like a man. I see him sleep
when he is not in need, fight when he *is* in
need; with nothing in his eyes but hunger,
lust, fury and fear,—but most of all fear.
His fellow animals do to him what they can;
the world of things does to him what it will,
or what it does not even will. What desires
he knows, and what of these he can satisfy,
are alike chance. Only the end of him is
not chance; it is physics, it is chemistry, it
is law of which he knows no more than that
it is older than he is.

Centuries pass. Those eyes are no longer
alternately clouded with lethargy and suf-
fused with passion. They are calm eyes,
"les yeux de science et de songe." And what
they look on is no longer a world of things
scattered by a wind that bloweth where it
listeth, but of things, at least a few things,
gathered and distributed as man has desired
them to be. His science has mastered the
law that is older than he is. To his art,
things have become plastic. He, Man, not
Fate, has become the potter; the world his
amphora.

Yet he has not wrought altogether well.
There is still some fear in those half-intelli-
gent eyes, the fear of his fellow-intelligence
that enters into rivalry with him in the in-
genious inventions of war and death. Why?

If you saw two children wrangling for a
penny at the very mouth of a treasure-cave,
would you not conclude they did not know?
So it is with us children of larger growth. I
venture to think a fraction of the intellectual
effort gone to the invention of such instruments of death as may acquire a few square
inches of coal-land for those who wield them

would ere now have harnessed wind and wave and the warm rays of the sun so to our service that a monopoly in coal lands would have come to interest us about as much as a corner in cemeteries. And so of all that war is waged for.

Must it not be, then, that men do not know? Would it be worth while to tell? I wonder.

Gentlemen, the story of my hopings for you has come to its term. I began by praying you might never be tempted to think, but left to enjoy, as some seem to enjoy, the beatitude of humdrumery. And when the thought struck me you were likely by this time past praying for, I was contrite. Yet if too late for this, not too late I trust for the next best bit of sound counsel. If you must think, at least think prudently. Accept your purpose in life from among the dozen or thousand or so that others about you and before you have found good enough. Invest a modicum of intelligence, if you feel you have it to spare, in gaining your object a little before the next man; but under

no circumstances let yourself ask whether
this object itself is worth gaining. Let your
motto be: What is good enough for others is
good enough for me. Do this, and you may
be reasonably sure that whatever life brings
you, it will be good enough for you.

But to the lost souls among you who will
not listen to prudence, but will insist on
thinking things out to the very end, let me
whisper this suspicion I have gathered from
my idle studies. Those who have thought
the end was nothing because they could see
no end of sameness, have not perhaps thought
far enough. Sameness *would* be eternal but
for such as you, dear fools. There is a
chance you may fool them yet with the crea-
tions of your folly. Now the name of this
folly is *Science;* that Science whose motto has
ever been

Mihi res, non me rebus, submittere conor.

Take it then for yours, if you will—with
the blessing of one who can think of no happier remeeting than what day you may return to claim—a fellow-fool.

MASTERY AND SERVICE

To the Philomathean Society

MASTERY AND SERVICE

It is well known that the philosopher has
two chief functions in life,—to make distinctions where no man can find a difference,
to deny difference where a world will be dying
for its distinctions. I do not know how it
comes that such a disturber of the peace
should have been allowed to abide so long
in the land, unless it be that life itself demands his service; or rather, that life demands of each man he shall hunt for the
hidden contradiction and feel for the secret
harmony of things. At the very beginning
of philosophy Heraclitus wrote, "The secret
harmony is better than the open." . . . But
you shall judge for yourselves.

Gentlemen, if I were to ask you, who are
about to enter upon serious adventures,
whether you would rather come out of them
a master or a servant, there could be no two

answers; for no man is willing to be servant if he have the strength to master. Why then, if I but change the wording, in a way which ought to make no difference in the sense of my question, will you at once divide into parties and thoroughly oppose one another? For whenever the world has asked itself which is nobler, the man who aims at mastery or he who aims at service, history shows the question to have split humanity in twain. On the one hand is the conquering majesty of imperial Rome; on the other the all-conquering gentleness of nascent Christianity. Or on the one hand is the captain of industry with his enormous control; on the other that patient soul who sees to it that certain slum-babies have a bit of ice to put their milk on and are not without milk to put on the ice.

This is not a vain distinction, is it? if the two ways of asking my question can bring such different responses. And all through life it is the same: he who would hold fast to the form of sound words has but one difficulty before him, to find the words that are sound. If you ask why this is, why men

have not yet learned to put thoughts into
words unequivocal, I can only suggest, it is
for no very long while this planet of ours
has turned and twisted its way among the
stars, and it is for only a little of this while
things have crept and crawled, things have
leaped and bounded on its surface. Only
very recently have some of these leaping
and bounding ones learned to balance themselves on their hind legs, and it is but yes-
terday certain of these hind-legged beings
took to uttering articulate speech and began
to misunderstand one another by word of
mouth. Is it surprising then if they still
lisp a little? That is why, wishing to discuss with you the world-old issue between
the life of mastery and the life of service,
it seemed important we should leave at the
threshold any prejudice we may have in favor
of being master rather than valet.

It is not of master and valet; it is of mastery and service we would speak. The difference between these two ideals is, you see,
real enough and important enough; as real
as the difference between that which is
Cæsar's and that which is God's; important

as having divided men in ancient times and as
dividing them no less to-day. The philosophers themselves recognize the reality of the
difference and take sides on it. The saintly
author of the *De imitatione* could not have
been more emphatic than was the philosopher
Schopenhauer in insisting that the love of
mastery is the root of all evil. Cæsar and
Napoleon could not have defended themselves as eloquently as the philosopher
Nietzsche defended them, nor would they
have put themselves as high as he put them.

What is good, what evil? asks Schopenhauer. Evil is that struggle of man to gain
mastery over nature and his fellows for the
fulfillment of his own desire. Good is the
abandonment of this struggle, the giving up
of the will to live, the unselfish, the selfless
life.

And "What is good?" asks Nietzsche.
"All that heightens in man the feeling of
power, the desire for power, power itself.

"What is bad?   All that comes from
weakness.

"What is happiness?   The feeling that

our strength grows,—that an obstacle is overcome.

"Not contentment, but more power; not universal peace, but war; not virtue, but forcefulness.

"The weak and ineffective must go under; first principle of *our* love of humanity. And one should even lend one's hand to this end.

"What is more harmful than any vice? Pity for the condition of the ineffective and weak—Christianity."

The Cæsarian conqueror and the Christian saint, the Schopenhauerian wiseman and the Nietzschean hero, can any difference between historic characters be more real? Can any contrast between ideals be more complete? Yet, I venture to think that this conflict, if it be taken to lie between the ideals of mastery and service, neither is nor can be real. No one can ever be called upon to choose between the life of mastery and the life of service, for the simple reason that no one can aim at either without aiming at the other; no one can master who does not also serve; no one can serve without mastering.

Why, yes, you say, that is after all quite true. A man must have mastered something before he can serve in any capacity, and a man must have served if he is to learn to master. The meanest valet must have mastered at least the art of matching odds and ends of haberdashery before he can find service. The highest king must have served in the hard, self-repressive school of prince-craft before he is permitted to rule. No one, from valet to king, who has not known both mastery and service. But, you say, the historic issue between mastery and service is really a question of outcome. The servant is he who ends a valet; the master he who comes out king; and this issue remains real and profound. To show that it is not so, it would be necessary to prove that each must *at the same time* be master and yet serve; serve and yet master!

Well, it is just this I meant to assert. It could be shown in any example of mastery and service you might choose to discuss; but every one will admit it without discussion for that most famous of battles between these ideals, the historic issue between self-mastery in the service of others on the one hand, domination over others to the end of self-aggrandizement on the other. Here there is no question of earlier and later: now and always I must aim at one or the other of these ideals, each of which is made up of both mastery and service.

This too, you allow, may be true enough; in all, as in this most important of historic conflicts between the idea of mastery and the idea of service, one must aim at the same time at mastering and serving. But if there is no longer a distinction between earlier and later, there is still a real difference between the ideals in question; for can one not well enough see that the parties are distinguished by their *ultimate* purpose: mastery, or service? And the great issue becomes, Which has the last word, mastery over men, or service of humanity? The pagan emperor, the Nietzschean hero, would subdue others to his service and call this mastery good. Christian saint and Schopenhauerian sage would down every impulse of his own nature, to spend his selfless life in others' service, and would call this life well spent.

This, you conclude, is the issue; it is real; it is historic; it is important.

It is certainly historic, I admit; and it is taken to be so important that our day and generation is inclined to offer as the mark of its highest civilization its firm acceptance of one and rejection of the other of these ideals. It can hardly be, gentlemen, that you who are by way of being orated into the full dignity of the baccalaureate will miss an invitation from one or another of your orators to spend the rest of your days in a noble striving to master yourselves and serve others. And yet, though I do not doubt your lives will be filled with noble deeds, I venture to predict that no one of you will accept this invitation, for the simple reason that no man could.

True, the "life of service" is commonly taken to stand for an important and historic theory of morals; but can you show me a single figure in all history whose practical philosophy could justly be summed up in this formula of self-suppression and service of others? Do not tell me that Christian saint or Schopenhauerian sage would afford

an example.   I do not mean merely that
history's saints are somewhat touched with
sin, and history's sages saved by a little folly.
But I mean that no one has really meant to
offer such final account of his life.   Not the
saint surely, else what is heaven for?
Heaven is the blessed haven where that self
which has for a little while denied and sup-
pressed its desires for others' sake shall at
last be satisfied and made replete.   The
philosophy of saintliness involves self-denial,
but it is a denial exercised here and now for
the sake of a fulfillment to come after while
and yonder.   As for the Schopenhauerian
sage, it was not indeed the promise of heaven
but the hope of death and forgetting which
made him praise the life of denial and value
the service of others more highly than the
satisfaction of self.   But this was only because the Christian heaven seemed to him
an improbable place and blessed eternity an
unlikely time.   Leaving these out, the only
remaining wisdom was to end the pain of life
in the best way.   The sage denied himself
in order to put pain from him; he served and
alleviated others because a sensitive sympa-

thy made their pain his own. Has he not then, granting his premises, striven to do the best for himself?

Do not think me pointing to an hypocrisy or insincerity in either saint or sage. I am merely illustrating the fact that it is not easy to express one's meanings, and that it is important to express them. Had I taken the Nietzschean hero instead of the Schopenhauerian sage for analysis, it would have been just as possible to show that the hero no more meant the domination of others to be his last word on life than the saint meant to exhaust the whole of himself in service. Indeed, Nietzsche was careful to explain that his hero's mastery was for the sake of some one other than the conqueror. It was at the feet of this other that the fruits of conquest, the very life of the conqueror, were to be laid:

"Higher than the love of thy nearest stands the love of those most remote from thee, thine offspring, the far-future man. Higher than the love of thy kind is for me the love of a Shadow. This Shadow that runs before thee is more beautiful than thou.

Why dost thou not give him thy flesh and thy bones?"

Shall we not conclude, then, that the difference between the ideals of service and of mastery is not after all real? Not merely because every one must both serve and master in the sense that one serves now in order to master then, or serves this in order to master that, but because at the very same moment and with respect to the very same thing all service involves mastery and all mastery service.

How can this be? you ask. But before we consider how it can be, let us assure ourselves by many examples that it is. These examples are not far to seek. We must master where we would serve, and if it is others we would serve, then these very others must we master! Ask any experienced physician how far he could expect to serve the patient he could not control. Ask any lawyer whether he could serve the client on whom he could not impose his guidance. Best of all, ask that wise and patient being, the old parish-priest or parson how much of his power to help depends upon his ability to master.

And there is a story of Kipling—who could not be accused of having left much of human nature unobserved; a story that has always seemed to me full of an unobtrusive philosophy. It tells of the troubles and perplexities of one who had been sent to relieve the famine-stricken province of Madras. In this land of death he arrived, "his carts loaded with wheat, millet, barley, good food-grains needing only a little grinding. But the people to whom he brought the life-giving stuff were rice-eaters. They knew nothing of the material that the white man conveyed so laboriously. They clamored for rice—unhusked paddy, such as they were accustomed to—and when they found that there was none, broke away weeping from the sides of the cart. In vain the interpreters interpreted, in vain his two policemen showed by vigorous pantomime what should be done. The starving crept away to their bark and weeds, grubs, leaves, and clay, and left the open sacks untouched. But sometimes the women laid their phantoms of children at his feet, looking back as they staggered away."

I dare say this servant of starving India is not the only one who has longed to thrash the man he is trying to serve and who will not be served. You will all of you have experienced this,—that much of the service of others bears a striking resemblance to the business of saving a drowning man or of taking home an obstreperous drunk. But it is part of the game, that if you undertake to serve you undertake to master too.

So at any rate our hero understood the game. But how master these foolish souls of Madras? One could not very well thrash starving men and women into eating barley when they were accustomed to rice. One could, though, get a starving mother of goats to eat of the barley starving mothers of men refused. One could persuade the now well-fed goat to give of her milk to the starving babies. "And when [so the story ends]—and when the women saw that their children did not die, they made shift to eat a little of the strange foods, and crawled after the carts, blessing the master of the goats." The

master of the goats had become through
them the master of his people, and only then
their savior. So much cunning mastery does
it take to be a servant of the ignorant of
one's kind!

Or I could tell another story not yet written in any book. Once upon a time on the
island of Atlantis there is said to have lived
a people rich, powerful, enlightened, who
had thoughtfully provided themselves, as
they explained to foreigners, with the best
form of government in the world. Some
think it may have been a republic, and for
the sake of the story let me call it so. However this may be, it is certain the people and
its government were inspired by the highest
ideals of peace and good will toward all men,
even their neighbors. They would conquer
none—at least, they would conquer no more
—and would help all to be happy and prosperous. As a natural consequence, the weaker
the neighbor and the more he had to profit
by this splendid idealism, the more he hated
the republic of my story. And there came
a time when one of these weaker ones was
torn by internal strife to which it seemed

there could be no end. Quick to spring to the help of others, our republic first placed itself between its helpless neighbor and the rest of the world; then it tried to place itself between the unhappy neighbor and the unhappy neighbor's self. Anxiously it watched, patiently it waited, and earnestly it hoped that it might be allowed to serve. Of those of its own people who lost their lives in the attempt to be useful, the republic said, "Beautiful is it to die in the service of one's country's neighbor."

But after a while that philosophy which is latent in the heart and brain of even the greatest idealist began to suggest to some in our republic that mere service, service which shrank from the responsibility of mastering, might have something wrong with it, —might turn out to be·an ideal indeed, but a lopsided ideal. The people began to remember experiences of saving drowning men who in their madness did everything to drown their rescuers with themselves. Some perhaps had had practice in the art of seeing Brugglesmith home. There began to be murmurs, "Policeman, do your duty!" . . .

But here the baffling tale breaks off. I do not know the end of the story, and I am sorry; for I think it might have given me another illustration of my thesis. I think its moral might have been: Do not undertake to serve unless you are prepared to fight for such mastery as will make your service possible.

Thus in many relations I have tried to show that the willingness to serve without the will to master is vain and null. But the converse would be just as true: Of the world's tyrants who have had real power over men, it might be said that the root of their power lay in their genius for serving; and that when this insight was lost, all attempts to maintain their mastery by imposing fear instead of giving service ended only in their undoing. The world tosses aside a Cæsar or a Napoleon as carelessly as it throws a used glove into the waste, sometimes indeed with a cruelty and ingratitude which shows how little it has understood its debt to the servant it has entrusted with mastership. It is no inappropriate thing that the royal house of England should have for its motto, "Ich dien." It is no untrue thing that was said by a president of this Republic, "I am your chief magistrate? Then am I the first of your servants." We who live in a day which is given over to revolt against certain forms of economic power may well learn from the example of this revolt that the man mistakes the extent of his real power who thinks it can go a hairsbreadth beyond the limits of his real service.

Gentlemen, I began by saying that I wished to show how necessary were the fine distinctions and bold reconciliations of philosophy to the understanding of very practical issues. As to the use you may make of this discourse, it will not be for determining what defines the higher life and what the lower. A wiser man than I, and one more confident, must be found to tell you this. There are some who have thought such distinctions as lie between general and private, employer and employed, master and servant to mean little in themselves, as marking off the high from the low. The emperor Marcus Aurelius and the slave Epictetus look very much on a level at this distance. There are some who have thought that if there be a last judge to evaluate our finite struggles we should not find in his judgment-book pages for the high and pages for the low, but perhaps only spaces for the upward-moving and spaces for the downward. But how are we to tell which is the upward way and which the downward? This, as I have said, is for a much wiser man than I to tell. I am content to have pointed out that some sign-posts in the land of morals have been wrongly inscribed, to the great misleading of the traveler. The road marked mastership and the road marked service seem to go in opposite directions. They do not, but form a circle that leads nowhere but to disillusionment and heartbreaking failure. These roads, then, I would have you erase from the mappemonde you take with you at the commencement of your journey.

Which you take with you at the commencement of your journey! I wonder whether you have ever thought what irony lies for us of the academic house in that word "commencement" which chance has chosen and tradition retained to mark the moment this occasion solemnizes.   I wonder whether you can imagine the impression left upon us of the house by the years-long rhythm of the "ave atque vale"?   Commencement, indeed! Well, it is that for you.   But for us it is one more shade added to the vague company of our memories,—until these minds of ours carry with them shadows lying "thick as autumnal leaves that strow the brooks in Vallombrosa."   Yet these memories, gentlemen, we would not be without.   And as few men, even when life is full in them, feel themselves to have mastered the things and served the purposes that once filled their vision, happen we find something more than solace in the thought that those who have called us master may somehow have found us serve.

OF COLLEGE SPIRIT AND
OTHER SPIRITS

To "The Red and Blue"

OF COLLEGE SPIRIT AND OTHER SPIRITS

Your middle-aged academic is likely to be an excellent gossip, and to enjoy more than other things connected with his profession the business of visiting his neighbors. His journey well behind him, whatever little formality has given excuse for his gadding disposed of well or ill, he is free to draw up to the fire with his colleague and let the quiet hours slip by. It is not of their respective universities these two talk; or if they do it is in the idle, detached, and amused way of men who have a whole universe to play in and little time for play. Yet somehow one seldom comes back from such wanderings without a new impression respecting the attitude of this or that other university toward one's own.

After one such occasion even pleasanter than others, I found myself rumbling home again with a new thought grumbling in my soul. "College spirit? They have no such thing. Pennsylvania knows nothing of what college spirit means." These remarks I had caught in passing. They had not been meant for me, and now they were mine I would willingly have been rid of their suggestion. They rumbled and, if you will, they rankled.

And, "What [I asked the first fellow-alumnus I came across on my return] do they mean? I had always thought the spirit of our university to be of the best; and it is not the only university in which I have lived. Nor you! You have migrated even more than I. Tell me what you think of this criticism."

"I think," he said, "it is true, but . . ."

I could not let him finish. "True?" said I. "You think it true the spirit of Pennsylvania is lacking? But it seems to me in several respects very superior indeed. In the first place we are not given to finding flaws in our neighbors. In fact we concern ourselves precious little with their domestic affairs; yet are not wanting in hospitality, I hope, when they give us the pleasure of receiving them. And then, as for ourselves, we like each other rather more than less and, if I know aught of these matters, are even willing to listen to the chap we like rather less than more if he have somewhat to say. The cleavages of social strata, of organizations, of creeds, races, complexions, and ways of parting the hair are less marked here than in other places you and I know of. Finally, to speak of purely scholastic things, the undergraduate impresses me as having hit on a fairly happy strain of seriousness tempered with humor. What, then, is the matter with the spirit of the college?"

"Nothing very vital is the matter with that spirit," said he. "Perhaps if the undergraduate were a trifle more serious the quality of his humor would not be spoiled. Or if his humor were more critical his appreciation of the serious might be a shade finer. (I say these things as in duty bound; for the Old Grad of our day said them of us, and the Older Grad of his day said them of him —such fine liturgical phrases must not be let perish for want of repeating.) However, you may recall that you stopped me on a *but.* You asked me if I thought we deserved the criticism of lacking college spirit. I said, 'Yes, *but—.*' Had you let me finish I should have rounded it out, 'Yes, college spirit is less pronounced here than elsewhere, but this is no unfavorable criticism.' "

"Develop me that," said I. "The matter promises to be curious."

"Curious?" quizzically. "But had you ever studied logic under a competent master, you would have learned to distinguish carefully between a horse-chestnut and a chestnut horse; so then you would not be surprised at this late day to find one admiring the spirit of a college just because it was lacking in college spirit."

"Nothing shocks me," I said, "and if you will explain to me how the spirit of the college can be the better for college spirit being the worse, I shall feel you will not have studied logic and such like sophistries in vain."

I shall try to tell you how this Old Grad argued the matter; but he was so confoundedly philosophical, I may have missed something of his meaning. If so, *tant mieux!*

"It all depends," he began, "on what you think of a Gesammtgeist."

This was a rather discouraging opening, for not only had I found it difficult to think of a Gesammtgeist at all (now a Gesammtgeist is a Collective Mind, if ever there was one)—not only had I found it difficult to think of a collective mind, but I had been so habitually perplexed in presence of any sort of mind, soul, spirit, or such like, I had found it better to hurry over any mention of them as fast and fluently as I could, that no one might have the chance to interpolate a question. Even the ordinary mind going about on its own two legs discoursing of war and the weather is hard to make out at times. "I don't see," said one such mind to me of a day, "how anybody can take the other side in this matter." "No more do I," spake my mind back to him. This harmony of sentiment was as near as we could come to understanding one another on a matter—which was *not* the weather. And it isn't only the other fellow's mind that is puzzling. There is a chap who has this long while been going about wearing my hat because he owns no

other, of whom the best I can say is that
perhaps if I knew him better I should think
a trifle more of him. It's an unfortunate
man who has to share his hat with the fellow who paid for it, but probably every one
of a certain age has come to know this mis-
ery.

Nevertheless I dare say we bipeds by
avoiding explanations should get along well
enough together, were it not for the philosophers. The philosophers have troubled matters by discovering our two-legged souls to
be not the only ones walking the earth. They
pretend, these philosophers, that there is
such a thing as a polypod soul, and even a
great variety of such. They insist that in
calling these spirits "collective minds" they
are only giving name to a class of entities
everybody knows and has had dealings with.
Do you find that you cannot live as you
want to because somehow you belong to a
larger whole, whose views of life are not
your views? Then the mind to which you
attribute these views that are not your views,
yet from whose compulsion you are not will-

ing to emancipate yourself, is what the philosopher calls a Gesammtgeist.

This sounds simple; but when our mind runs on to examples we find difficulties. "Do you mean to tell me," I once put it to the philosopher, "that the young aspirant to art or the sighing lover who finds a family council barring his way to the blessed life has come in contact with a collective mind? Isn't there a difference between a collection of minds and a mind collective?"

"Yes," the philosopher amplified his thought, "there is all the difference in the world between these two things. The man whose voice is drowned in many voices will not have heard a Gesammtgeist speaking. The many voices produce an aggregate of noise, rather loud than persuasive. The voice of the many is still, small, and very cogent.

"Maybe there *is* a collective mind to be called Family Sentiment, but it would need no council to voice its meanings. Have you never come across a group of beings the fundamental postulate of whose existence was their common relationship to one great-grandfather? (But the kinsmen I have in mind are modern, emancipated, a little Saninesque.) Imagine Cousin Peter inviting Cousin Paul, Cousin Kate and the rest to dinner, to announce his engagement to his housemaid! There is not one of them but would clap him on the back and compliment him on his good sense and originality. The funny part of it is that, although quite sure of this, Cousin Peter would never think of assembling the great-grandchildren of his great-grandfather to receive their blessings. Why not? He would know all the while that the collective mind of the family had no part nor share in the many-voiced applause. It would be mute, this ghost, for since dear downright Aunt Jane was no more it would be left no tongue to speak with; but its silent presence at the feast would be felt by all foregathered.

"No," my philosopher ran on, "the power of the polypod spirit is not the power of numbers; the collective mind is not a collection of minds. Do you suppose a mob in the days of the Terror was composed of monsters? Do you not rather believe Cito-

yen Chose to have been much the same genial
bonhomme then we know him for to-day?
How by adding sheep can you produce a
tiger? But given the conditions, you can
witness the aggregate feet of the flock rush-
ing on with the soul of a tiger."

Many would seem to be the forms in
which the collective mind appears to philosophy. Now it is Family Sentiment, now
Public Opinion, Call of Country, Voice of
Nature. And again it is that less serious but
still interesting thing we call "College
Spirit." Whether you value and strive to
cultivate college spirit, "all depends," my
friend would have it, "on what you think of
a Gesammtgeist."

What I am sure of is that, had any one
put this issue to the undergraduates of my
day, he would have received different answers under different conditions.

Had he taken each man aside and put to
him, "What, after all, are you here for? Is
it to help cultivate a spirit that shall continue to cheer long after you have lost all
voice to cheer with? Or are you here to

grow strong of your own strength, so that
when college spirit shall have become as
vague and forgotten a thing to you as a kiss-
ing game at kindergarten you will still be
using and know you are using the eternal
science or the everlasting art you are strug-
gling for here and now, as who should say,
between cheers?"—had he put the matter
in this way, not a man of us but would have
said to himself, "I came here alone, alone
must I go forth again. Only new power can
go with me out of these doors. For what
but that new power am I within them?"

But had he gathered us all together and
orated, "Fellows, what are you here for?
Is it to add a little to your private stock of
wisdom, or is it to push this great university
on to glory?"—we should have cheered to
a man, sung the Marseillaise, damned the in-
dividualist, and helped somebody to win a
football game or two—at the cost of his very
life if need be. The collective spirit would
have had us, and we should have been glad
in it.

These two attitudes toward university or
universe seem fairly contradictory. Not but

what there are some amiable souls who would remove all difficulties by suggesting "a little of both"; enough getting off by oneself to see the university as no more than an episode in a whole life; enough losing of concern for self to know what it means to live for The Whole. I say, there are many who have thought this a reasonable and satisfactory solution of the puzzle facing every man who has come to ask himself, "Is the world my oyster? Or am I but a morsel for the world's consumption, that it may live?" He is invited to answer himself, "A little of both," or, "Just enough of each, please."

Now I dare say the true solution will make it out that life in a university and life in the universe must combine something of using and something of being used. But how much? A little of both? Just enough of each? Such measures of proportion are all we want in a recipe for cocktails. They give the genial sinner a chance for once to score one on the saintly. There is something sporting in the formula we are not altogether averse to. But how mix in tasteful measure life and death? Suppose our *universitas* to be our country, and suppose us called on to decide between giving life for country or yielding country for life's sake?   And at the moment when this issue faces us, suppose our amiable reconciler to come along with his favorite recipe, Try a little of both.   Does that mean, Die a little while you run a little? Or, Run first then come back and die?   Or, Die first then run awhile?   The thing seems hard to manage any way you put it.

So it is that more serious-minded beings have aimed not at a compromise between the mind of the whole and the mind of the part, but at a reasoned subjection of one to the other.   Some would call this the struggle between the *soul of loyalty* and the *spirit of liberty;* and although such sounding names are generally unsound we may consider the issue in somewhat these terms.

We other Americans are a money-grubbing lot, altogether given over to materialism.   We know this, for our neighbors have been uniformly candid in calling the matter to our attention.   And besides, our own observation should show us how right they are.

For if the recent history of Europe is to be looked upon as a struggle of idealists for their ideals, then have we been lacking in such ideals. Instead of minding our business in a pettifogging way, we might have been extending the benefits of our culture to those whose want of it was entirely proven by their not wanting it. Had we done this and assured the world we meant to keep on doing it, we might have qualified for participation in that strenuous life which is just now dying for its ideals.*

How beautiful, then, must be the idea which can make even our cold natures glow, —*Pro patria mori!* For, if I remember, our eyes were very young when first they made out dim brothers moving glorious in the mists of Thermopylæ. Our hearts had not been long a-beating before they felt the spear-points Arnold von Winkelried gathered to his breast. Our feet were tender enough when they left new stains on the snows of Valley Forge,—and our spines will have grown very stiff when neither Yankee Doodle

* The reader will please imagine himself back with us in the Fall of 1914.

nor Dixie can send another chill down them.

And who knows but that, occasion offering, we might not go beyond this admiring
of brave gifts men have given to their countries long ago? Perhaps we too could give
and have that joy in giving which is the only
thing can make such giving possible. For not
for abstract principles of duty nor for love
of present applause or of posthumous fame
can men be made to do such things. The day
is past when men "wooed war as a mistress,"
and this joy or enthusiasm or madness in giving can be nothing but the voice of a
Gesammtgeist crying out in us. Is not then
this collective soul a very noble soul, far
above yours and mine, and one into which we
should at all times encourage ours to merge?
And as preparation for such merging, is not
the habit of organizing our biped selves into
polypod groups a wise and useful thing? Is
not, for example, the worth of a college to
be measured by the strength of its college
spirit?

But I should not say the only reason for
cultivating a sense of membership lies in
the training it provides in the art of self-

sacrifice. The collectivity has much to offer in return for what it asks. There seems to be a type of man who can do nothing effective unless he feel The Organization back of him. His first affair in life is to rush to join something. Nor does he by preference select such loose associations as city clubs, which having no cause to live for would have no cause for living did they not make easy the meeting and companionship of two-legged souls. But this man wants compact organization; his soul loves to be carried along on many feet marching in rhythm. He enjoys only what he can do as one of a crowd; the "coming on untasted springs, the gathering of new flowers"—these things tempt him not, for the unshared and new means to him the lonely and unattached. Some of this timidity before untried things is in the heart of the bravest of us, and many a man who would charge with his troop would rather not be alone in the dark. Yes, the Gesammtgeist knows how to give as well as to take, and are not its giving and its taking of an order higher than the personal winnings and losings of the man-by-himself?

In some such way as this I tried to lay before my friend the claims of the Gesammt-geist to our allegiance, to our "spirit of loyalty."

"You have argued," said he, "with an eloquence that does credit to your sentiment, but hasn't your review of history overlooked some little episodes? While your eyes were straining to make out through their tears the Spartans dying at Thermopylæ, mine had shifted on to a figure that, after having sent the women away and said his say to his friends, accepted the cup Athens offered him as a reward for his personal adventures in the domain of thought. And while your heart was bleeding on Austrian spears, mine was feeling that point which pierced the side of a lonely figure on a cross, a cross the spirit of his race had given him in return for glad tidings of new things he had brought. While you were freezing at Valley Forge, I was burning at the stake to which Christendom had tied that poor philosopher who first imagined the distant stars to be other suns; who revived lost memories of an infinite world uncentered in man. If the Volksgeist has made a music that thrills with the soul of this great ghost, what other music of what other beauty and thought has been made by fiddler or poet forlorn in his attic! We do not know much of high and low perhaps; but so far as we know anything, would you venture to claim the high things of history for the collective spirit rather than for what daring has strayed from the herd on its private provision of legs? What if you do find a few great impersonal monuments rising like Gothic cathedrals above the dead level of common thought and deed, are these not more than offset by the wonderful and exquisite things The People has trodden underfoot?

"You speak," my friend went on, "of the supporting power of collectivity that holds up him who stumbles and coddles him in its everlasting arms. But isn't there some danger in giving up your own strength to these protecting arms? Hasn't it happened on occasion that the Protector of the Poor has forgotten he was *for men*, come to think of men as being *for him*, and of himself as More-than-Man, as Empire?"

And my friend recalled a recent picture (entirely fanciful, let us suppose) of one such Imperial Mind whose imagination had been fired by a new philosophy of the Mailed Fist:

"Full of the confidence and lordliness of youth, it was the youngest philosophy that the world had seen since the days of the Greeks; it made no concession whatever to the intellectual toryism of old age, the timidity and inertia of so-called experience. And if it was thus young and perhaps even a bit juvenile, then let us not forget that its Country was young too. Here indeed was the youngest of all the great nations, the baby among the powers. The winds of great adventure were still sharp and spicy to its nostrils; it felt the swelling of its muscles, the itch of its palm on the sword hilt; and it gazed out upon the world proudly, steadily, disdainfully. And here of its own blood was a philosopher who gave validity, nay, the highest validity to its impulses, its appetites, its ambitions. Here was one who drove a lance through the Beatitudes, and hung a new motto upon the point: 'Be hard!'

"Barbarous?   Ruthless?   Unchristian?
No doubt.   But so is life itself.   So is all
progress worthy the name."

"But," I interrupted, "do you not love this
playful young thing your poet has so sym-
pathetically and eloquently evoked for us?"

"Perhaps," said my friend, "I like least in
my poet what is best in his art—a certain
verisimilitude.   If we were quite sure that
nothing but ink had been spilled by the
'Prophet of the Mailed Fist' . . . !

"But it was not to find fault with his
poetry or its hero that I introduced my poet.
It was rather to show how curiously the
romantic mind works when it tries to reason,
and particularly when it comes to reason about
minds collective and distributive.   For after
while comes the inevitable question, Is this
gaillard Spirit to prevail?   And here my poet
answers: 'Let us not assume his downfall too
lightly.   And let us not be alarmed by his
possible triumph.   What did Rome ever produce to match the Fifth Symphony?' "

He came to a full stop, as though an ob-
vious point had been scored.

"But," I ventured, "what *is* the point?"

"Why," said he, "it seems to me the symphony in question was written by an uncollected person who luckily for us lived at a moment in That Country's history when no fine young Gesammtgeist was going through the land looking for material in which to express *its* idea. Had this person waited a century to be born, he might have been part of that material. It is doubtful whether the idea he would then have served to express were better worth expressing than the ones he had the chance to write down for us before the Imperial Spirit awoke. Your glorious young Empire is just the sort of thing that makes your glorious old writer of symphonies improbable. But Empire for Empire, there is this to be said for the Roman: it had the gumption to come on the scene several centuries before the fall of Rome, rather than many after."

"My dear fellow," I said, "a long while ago I asked you a simple question about the lack of college spirit at Pennsylvania; and now, after having traipsed up and down the universe with me panting after, would you mind telling me in a word or two what you think about this lack of spirit you so frankly admit?"

"Well," said he, "in one word, It all depends on what you think of a Gesammtgeist!"

As we were walking home he suddenly broke an enjoyable and well-earned silence to ask a question. "By the way," said he, "have you met many graduates of colleges in which college spirit is well-developed?"

"Some few," I recalled.

"And how did they impress you?"

After thinking them over, they "seemed to me all alike pleasant fellows."

"All alike pleasant, yes. But," he hesitated, "aren't they painfully all-alike?"

While I was revolving this, I heard him mutter something to himself. I thought he said, "Their souls need too· many feet to walk on."

After which he puffed his pipe and relapsed into a silence from which I was careful not to draw him. There's no getting sense out of these philosophers, you know.

"DEATH OF THE WESTERN
WORLD"
and
"THE MARTYRDOM OF MAN"

To the Modern Literatures Club

"DEATH OF THE WESTERN WORLD"
and
"THE MARTYRDOM OF MAN"

It is a pleasant and not ungenerous custom of men who read to pass on word of their readings, whereby the fame of good books is the quicker spread and unprofitable hours oneself has spent spared another's wasting. One who to this manner of gossip has owed many a new friend, escaped doubtless many an old bore, is only too glad of permission to contribute his item of news.

His item of news! That last word holds me suspended. To tell of some new thing is no hard task, but can my latest novelty boast that spice without which the newest thing is none too newsy? Or again, I happen recently to have been retasting a bit of older spice; should the remoteness of its first offering exclude it from current comment, even though there is a sad newness to the justice done this long-neglected thing? I wonder.

So wondering, after having accepted your invitation to address the Club, I was inspired of a rather happy thought. It occurred to me I could not well miss both novelty and spice if of the two works contending in my mind I chose—both. Which decided, the choice began to take on unforeseen merits, as one's random decisions so often will if properly encouraged. Of which merits the one I was happiest to discover sprang from the kindred themes of the two volumes. Both indeed were preoccupied with the same large mouthful of gossip; namely, the history of the world. But taking it this way and taking it that, the two had managed to make of this same world such opposite things, it would I saw be enough to lay them side by side to make each the other's critic. So might your reviewer, idle showman of others' wit, preserve his own urbanity in a world whose mood, whatever else it might be, was clearly most contentious.

My two volumes deal, as I have said, in that same bit of gossip called "Universal History," a subject sometime fallen into dis-

repute with minds whose entire stock of seriousness was invested in the single care of
accuracy. But lately, it would seem, the
catching of history's total sweep has recov-
ered some dignity as a task, and in the per-
formance of a Wells or a Van Loon won new
popularity. In this is little wonder, for
though we can no longer feel Augustine's
thrill in recognizing history's divine culmination; though we cannot recover Hegel's
solemnity in following history's dialectic
through its endless unfolding, yet we still
turn over in our minds at times certain mag-
nificent questions. Whether this humanity
staggering on be really tending somewhither,
or whether it be not running round in very
circular circles, or whether it have not to
keep urging its pace just to stay where it has
been? And we naturally suppose human history, did we but get enough of it, should yield
us some hint of an answer. How should we
not be grateful then to a writer who has the
temerity to tackle a problem so hopelessly
vast no modest soul could assume it? And
then in the end there is always the fun of
showing the egregious blunder this fellow

revolving a world in his head made, page
four hundred and twenty.

But this luxury of scrutinizing details I
leave as a sort of enticement to those who
if they would join in the sport must at least
turn some of the pages. As for me, I am
content with the whole, the Idea and what
may come of it. Or rather, we are to have
two Ideas; but I will tell first of the newer—

I

"DER UNTERGANG DES
ABENDLANDES"

To this "Death of the Western World"
its author, Oswald Spengler, has given a
modest subtitle: it is to be but an "Introduction to a Morphology of World-His-
tory." * Such a plan must begin with a
sweep, but the author reserves for the last
what he calls his "narrower theme." If he
searches the world as a whole, it is in order
to find some answer to a homely intimate
question, What is to become of *Us?* "Us,"

* Der Untergang des Abendlandes, *Umrisse einer Mor-
phologie der Weltgeschichte,* Erstes Band: *Gestalt und
Wirklichkeit.* München, 1920.

in its most hospitable mood, stretches itself
to include not only all Western Europe but
the Europeanized New-World as well.
Principally though the author's thought is of
his German People; and if we are allowed
part in their fate, it is because we share their
"culture." (This, we shall presently see, is
no very hopeful omen.)

Now whatever interest the philosophy of
the whole must have for any one, any time,
am I wrong in supposing us closer to its "narrower theme" at this moment? I may then
do no more than bring in easy relation with
a vast conception of destiny Spengler's specific answer to the more specific question.

Since the days when Nebuchadnezzar
dreamed and Daniel had "visions of his head
upon his bed," we have been more or less
accustomed to behold the kingdoms of this
earth as mortal man or beast or both, sharing
with man and beast the prospect of undoing.
Only, the ways of life and death have
changed with the lapse of ages. In those old
days, death was commonly so violent a thing
we are not surprised to find the prophet ex-

pecting the death of one beast at the teeth
and claws of another. But in our milder
times it is natural that those who reflect on
the mortality of kingdoms should think of
the manner of their taking-off as more in the
likeness of a sickening and dying-from-
within than of battle, murder and sudden-
ness. . . .

"To the one cause [wrote Winwood Reade,
some fifty years ago] may be traced the ruin
and the fall not only of Egypt, but of all the
powers of the ancient world; of Nineveh,
and Babylon, and Persia; of the Macedonian
kingdom and the Western Empire. As soon
as these nations became rich they began to
decay. If this were the fifth century and
we were writing history in the silent melancholy streets of ancient Rome, we should
probably propound a theory, entirely false,
yet justified at that time by the universal
experience of mankind. We should declare
that nations are mortal like the individuals
of which they are composed; that wealth is
the poison, luxury the disease which shortens
their existence and dooms them to an early
death." (A "false theory," Reade calls it;

but all he had come to regard as false in this theory of nations' natural death was the hasty diagnosis: not riches but unequal distribution of riches was the fatal disorder to which succumbed these imperial "men outworn.")

Well, Spengler has in his turn come upon the conception of "Kulturen" as *persons*. With a naïveté difficult to explain in a man of his overwhelming lore, he is beyond measure impressed with the originality of this insight. Not indeed as a gesture of personal vanity does he insist again and again on the regeneration of history this new compelling idea must accomplish—rather is there something apostolic in the simplicity and sincerity of his enthusiasm. But no matter for that— and for that matter there *is* something new in his interpretation of these culture-lives: it is his theory of their dying. For not by violence, nor by possibly avoidable poison or conceivably preventable disease do they die; but just of that most fatal of all internal disorders, *old age*. And the name of old age is—*civilization!*

In the last paragraph the portentous word

fate crept on us unannounced—yet it is *the* word of the Death of the Western World. But if unannounced, this fate (Schicksal) cannot have come on us unexpected. We had been speaking of life; and of life, is not its birth fatal and do not all who are born "stagger [as Schopenhauer has put it] through the four ages of life to death," fatally bound for that goal? Wherefore, if the cultures of India, of Greece, of Arabia, of Western Europe are indeed "persons," then however different their "physiognomies," they must even spend themselves in similar ways to the same end and conclusion.

"Every culture [writes Spengler] runs through the ages of an individual man. Each has its childhood, its youth, its prime, its senility. A young, shyly divining soul reveals itself in the morning-time of the Romanic and Gothic period; it fills the Faustian landscape from the Provence of the Troubadours to Bishop Bernward's Hildesheim. Here blows the wind of spring! A like childhood speaks in the kindred tones of early Homeric Doric, of Late Christian art, and in the works of Egypt's Old Kingdom.

In all these a mythical world-sense struggles
with what is dark and dæmonic in itself and
in nature about it as with a thing of sin,
slowly maturing the while toward a pure
luminous expression of personality won and
grasped. . . .

"At first all is cramped, confused, tenta-
tive, full of childish wistfulness and childish
timidity. (Recall the church doors of
Saxony, of Southern France; consider the
Dipylon vases.) But now in full consciousness of ripe power (as in the age of Sisostris,
of the Pisistratidæ, of Justinian I, of
Charles V's Spain) all the details of expression are controlled, severe, measured, of a
wonderful lightness and intelligibility. Here
we find everywhere instances of luminous
perfection; influences that brought into being
the Hypsos Sphinx of Tanis, the dome of
St. Sophia's, the painting of Titian.

"Later—delicate, almost fragile, melancholy with the sweetness of late October
days—are the Aphrodite of Gnidus, the
Chorus Hall of the Erechtheon, the ara-
besques of the Saracen arch, the "Dresdener
Zwinger,"—Watteau, Mozart.

"At last—in the stage of senility we call civilization—the soul-fire is extinct. A declining vigor makes one more effort at creation—with only half-success: Classicism, stranger to no dying culture; Romanticism, a weary soul thinking back on its childhood. Then tired, disillusioned, and cold, it relaxes its hold on existence and longs—as in Roman times—to return out of the light back into the darkness of soulless mysticism, back to the mother's lap, to the grave. Herein was the spell the cults held for dying Rome— those of Isis, Serapis, Horus, Mithras—the same cults a soul just then awakening in the East was making the first dream-like timid expression of its Being and was filling with new meaning."

There is, what I should think would be a melancholy fascination for our author in scrutinizing the "physiognomy" of these heroic figures as they pass, in divining the culture-soul beneath historic gesture. But what is deepest in this or any soul is its attitude toward the coming-into-being and passing-away of things, toward Sein and Werden. India would fain have forgotten both Sein

and Werden to lose itself in Nichtsein—
Nirvana. Egypt could not forget; with a
passion for remembering, it eternalized in
the tomb what time would have let perish.
The Antique (Græco-Roman) spirit, ab-
sorbed in the luminous here and now was
without perspective of time or space: Der
Grieche niemals wurde, sondern immer war
(12). Alone among all, the Modern (Western European) soul has caught that deep
sense of participation in a larger life, which
makes it ever seek its meaning in what lies
beyond. Wistfully, like a note in some musical strain, its moment hangs suspended between what went before and what is yet to
come.

It is in showing how the undertone of its
soul is to be felt in every expression of a
culture that Spengler spends what I have
called his "overwhelming lore." Yet, as I
have said, the fascination this task has for
him must be a somber one. For as we watch
the great cultures come and go, however
inspired—whether of Nichtsein, Sein, or
Werden—they pass on their fatal way, nor
leave anything behind by which others better

than they might come to conquer fate. Do I say they leave nothing? They have left the record of their having been, from which the modern soul imbued with the spirit of history may not indeed conquer but, better than any who have gone before, know the ways of destiny . . .

"A horizonless throng of humanity, a shoreless flood out of a past too dark for the sense of time to order, where restless troubled fancy gropes in a witch's dream of geological periods behind which lies a riddle past finding out, losing itself again in an equally timeless future—this is the medium whereover the forms of history pass. With the monotonous wave-rhythm of countless generations, its vast surface moves. Over it great cultures send out their majestic rings. Of a sudden appearing, their splendid contours spread, subside, disappear; and the mirror-like surface of the deep lies sleeping solitary as before." (153)

In the light of such a vision of the whole, we approach the author's "narrower theme" —this Western world of ours.

Everything about our Western world shows it to be civilized; which is to say, near its latter end. But nothing is more revealing than is that dream Germany did but now dream the deepest,—*Imperialism*. From depth of feeling and conviction, our author's words ring magisterially out: "I teach," he cries—

"Here I teach that we must look upon imperialism as the typical symbol of passing away. Its petrified remains may endure for centuries and millennia handed on from one conquering fist to another—so it was with the kingdoms of Egypt, China, Rome, with the Indian world and Islam. But dead bodies were these remains; amorphous, soul-bereft masses of men; the used material of great histories. Imperialism is civilization pure, in whose [contemporary] manifestation is revealed beyond gainsaying the fate of the Western world." (51)

One recalls the famous phrase of Maximilian Harden, "Wir haben es gewollt!" This is the spirit those find in Nietzsche who hail him "Prophet of the Mailed Fist." How different appears the gigantic thing

Harden's people had "willed" to the reflec-
tive, retrospective gaze of Spengler!

Expansion! it is the master-word of imperialism. "It expresses the most character-
istic tendency of every matured civilization,
of the Roman, the Arabic, the Chinese.
Here is no room for choice; here the conscious will neither of the individual nor of
whole classes and peoples decides the issue.
The expansive tendency is a thing of destiny, a thing dæmonic and non-human
(Ungeheures) seizing the late comer on the
world-stage, compelling him into its service,
using him whether he will or no, whether
he know or not." And our author adds by
way of a note: "The modern Germans are
the shining example of a people who without
knowing or willing it became expansionist.
They were already so in the days when they
thought themselves Goethe's people. Bis-
marck never so much as suspected this deeper
meaning in the epoch he founded; he be-
lieved himself come to the end of a political
development." (52)

One cannot have followed Spengler so far
without wondering what last word he will

have for *the individual* caught in this fatal life-trend of a Kultur. It would, I think, be this:

"Who cannot understand that of this conclusion nothing may be modified, that a man must will this or nothing at all, that we must love this destiny or despair of the future and of life; who cannot feel the bigness of Reality as the higher intelligence sees it, of the energy and discipline of iron-hard natures, of this struggle with the coldest and abstractest of media; who goes about with the idealism of a provincial, mourning the life of days gone by—such an one must give up hope of understanding history, of living history, of making history."

Perhaps, after all, here is a way of reconciling the "Wir haben es gewollt" of Harden and the "We neither knew nor willed; but now that we know, *ought* to will" of Spengler. It is the self-dedication of the Imperial Stoic, "Thy will be my will, O Destiny."

Such is the world, and such the Death of the Western world. I offer no comment or criticism—as how or why should one spend

science on what is after all a learned poem?
For "the poet [our author has written] and
the historian are one; the mathematician and
scientific thinker, another." Intuition, the
sympathy that gives to the human heart as
it beats a deep and inexplicable insight into
all hearts that have beaten—whether of particular men or of multitudinous cultures—
this is the author's organ of historical appreciation. With such mystical methods, who
can quarrel or to what purpose?

But if I offer no historian's comment on
this conception of history's facts, as philosopher and man I reserve the privilege of quar-
reling with the author's interpretation of
their ethical meaning for you and for me.
This interpretation as you see is based on
the familiar assumption, seeming to some of
us so pitiable, that a human being is more
truly and profoundly a part of some social
organism than he is a two-legged entity with
a life of his own to make or to mar and a
cause of his own to elect. Now if you were
an individual convinced that the fates had
brought you to your birth as one of an outworn people dying of their civilization,

would you bow your head and murmur,
"Thy will be my will, O Destiny! Thy fate
be my fate, O Higher Unity; O Type of
Civilization!"?

I trow not. The first thing you would ask
yourself would, I think, be this: Is there
nothing that goes on and on in the world
though men, nations, races, cultures cease and
perish? And if you found such an imper-
ishable thing, one unbroken life evolving
through all history, would you not rather
leave your Kultur to its civilization and yourself cling to life—*this* life?

There are those who think they find this
eternal life running through the passing cul-
tural phases of history. With all it has to
tell of perishing and vanishing, *history has
never told that Science dies.* Science? It is
the torch runner hands on to runner, though
each fall exanimate as the precious thing is
snatched from his slackening fingers. And as
it goes, it grows.

There are those who have thought of history in this way: of one of them, let me tell
an old, and somewhat sad, and somewhat
beautiful tale.

"THE MARTYRDOM OF MAN"

In 1879, there died at Wimbledon, England, a man who dying may well have felt he could look back on a life of as well-wasted years as thirty-five gave time for. All he had set his heart on turned ashes, or was snatched from him. "Heir to considerable estates which he did not live long enough to inherit, he was gifted with a genius he had no time to mature." In these words his famous uncle, Charles Reade, sums up his story.

And yet all the active part of these thirty-five years was spent in one ceaseless struggle, almost breathless to attain—what? Fame! fame that should be immortal and a name all men should know. To do what no man had done before, to go where no man had gone: this fire consumed him. We can see there was a moment when almost he was content. At a point of the river Niger a hundred miles higher than any European had attained, before returning to Freetown and the home of civilization he sings a Nunc dimittis to the Wilderness around. In his "African Sketch Book" we find him recording, "Henceforth no man can say I am only a writer: for I have proved myself a man of action as well as a man of thought. When in the morning I have taken my coffee which sets my brain in a tremble and a glow, I walk along the red path, and as the country unfolds before me I say, 'This is mine: here no European has been; it is Reade's Land.' " (xx)*

But it was not, exactly; for it proved not to be Fame. All his life long was Winwood Reade striving to reach the real "Reade's Land." He sought it first in the world of letters: no one read his "Charlotte and Myra," his "Liberty Hall," his "Veil of Isis" —no one, except the critics. These in their journals damned his output as fast as put out. It is described as consistently insolent, pertinaciously *anti*, which is to say, against sound traditions of University, Church, Society. For the rest, it was very bad fiction; its characters voiced the sentiments of one impudent

* *The Martyrdom of Man,* twenty-second edition, with an Introduction by F. Legge, London.

fellow Reade; they did that, and nothing
more. And after having never existed they
flatly refused to survive.

This was before 1862: then came new
things. Darwin had written his "Origin of
Species" in 1859; our adopted fellow-Ameri-
can, Paul du Chaillu, had brought back the
tales which in 1861 filled his "Explorations
and Adventures in Equatorial Africa, with
Accounts of the Manners and Customs of the
People, and of the Chace of the Gorilla,
Crocodile, and Other Animals." In your
imagination, bring these two things together:
the problem of remote origins; the mists of
primeval forests! What in the way of
origins might not these dark forests retain,
these tropical mists cover? The "origin of
species" had been told, but what of the
origins of Mind? Where these might be
found preserved in jungles closed to all but
the hero—might not *there* be a place its
finder could well call His Own?

Thither went Winwood Reade, and there
through adventures too long and too many
to tell he did really wonderful things.
There he all but left his life, and did leave

all his health. With boundless audacity, with no prudence, no foresight, no plan, he wandered on to meet what he might meet. The things he did were important; commercial England profited by the trade routes he opened; later exploration traveled far on the knowledge he gained. Much he did for the good and fame of others, for his own good and his own fame he knew not how to plan. He who did all things for fame, saw no fun in doing the one thing that would doubtless have made him famous. He brought back with him no cold observations, no such scientific records as might have claimed the attention of (say) the Royal Geographical. This "man of action" told of his actions as though he was "only a writer": he made of them a story. No land came to be "Reade's Land," for all his heavy toil.

What matters the rest of this life? More travels: war-correspondent in the Ashanti, a correspondent who not to be idle fought in the ranks of the Black Watch; more bad romans à clef, this time directed against the "superstition" of Christianity. Then death: that was all,—except a dream.

Raymond Jenoure (the hero of Reade's romance "See-Saw") at one time avows his intention of painting a series of pictures portraying the passions and their influence, of traveling in foreign countries to observe the manners and customs of other, and especially savage, peoples. Then, says he, "should I ever live to carry out these two gigantic designs, having by that time read all the great books, studied all the great languages, traveled everywhere and seen everything, I shall begin to write the *History of the World*." (xxvi)

Our "Raymond Jenoure" (otherwise Winwood Reade) may not have traveled everywhere, but farther than most; he may not have read everything, but more than enough; he was by way of getting all ready for his "History of the World"—when he died. Instead of this great epic, he left a little story, a sort of sketch—no more. Yet H. G. Wells in the opening of his *Outline of History* takes this "Martyrdom of Man" to have been date-making in the history of History. For Reade it was a by-product, of which we may imagine the only part he prized was the part all his friends urged him to omit. This was the philosophical conclusion: his very firm conviction that "Christianity must go." Need we say that appearing in these early seventies, flaunted in Victorian England's unspeculative eye, the "Martyrdom of Man" was quite there to be martyred? Never until recently has the book received favorable review, notice, comment, or appreciation. Yet in our day it has found for its dead author an eminence the living Reade never knew he came to, never did set out for,—a sort of pensive Reade's Land peculiarly his own.

Recall if you will Spengler's conception of history, a sequence of culture-lives, each with its personal physiognomy, each leaving behind it a record of having been—and leaving nothing more. Alongside this we would lay a vision of humanity's life as one; one growing in stature and wisdom and in favor with God-in-Man. The spirit animating this life is groping, experimental—questioning, it works on the mechanism about it to subdue this to its will, on the human material of its own body that it may come to know health.

Its history is a history of mistakes, of very painful blunders; but if its experience has hurt, has it not also enlightened?

"If we compare the present with the past, if we trace events at all epochs to their causes, if we examine the elements of human growth, we find that Nature has raised us to what we are, not by fixed laws, but by expedients, and that the principle which in one age effected the advancement of a nation, in the next age retarded the mental movement, or even destroyed it altogether. War, despotism, slavery, and superstition, are now injurious to the progress of Europe, but they were once the agents by which progress was produced." (502)

To show the origin, promise, fallacy, failure of man's experiments—war the energizer, nationality the organizer, class rivalry the stimulator, and world-welding religion—to show these in temporal order is one part of history; and this part gives its name to "The Martyrdom of Man." But to show this painful thing to have been no mere waste suffering; to show these mistakes to have been indeed the "agents by which progress has been produced"; to show in all this "progress" more than change of fashion,— this if it be not history must be something more.

If it was as "poet" Spengler felt his way into the heart of cultures, it is as poet-painter Reade lets one share his vision of the past:

"We have traced the stream of history to its source in the dark forest; we have followed it downwards through the steppes of the shepherds, and the valleys of the great priest peoples; we have swept swiftly along, past pyramids and pagodas, and the brick-piles of Babylon; past the temples of Ionia, and the amphitheaters of Rome; past the castles and cathedrals lying opposite to mosques with graceful minarets and swelling domes; and so, onwards and onwards, till towns rise on both sides of the stream; towns sternly walled, with sentinels before the gates; so, onwards and onwards, till the stream widens and is covered with ships large as palaces, and towering with sails; till the banks are lined with gardens, and villas; and huge cities, no longer walled, hum with industry, and becloud the air; and deserts or barren hills are no longer to be seen; and the banks recede and open out like arms, and the earth-shores dissolve, and we faintly discern the glassy glimmering of the boundless sea." (491, 2)

Beyond the mouth of this river, over the unknown waters which outlie the Present, speculation surveys the courses man has yet to run. But such speculation would be blind, had contemplation discovered no tendency of the past by whose line projected new courses might be laid.

Not as a last "expedient" for the first time lately tried, but as a suspicion dawning with mankind, feeding on its failures, growing with defeat, claiming at last direction of all life undertakes, runs a patient spirit the name of which is *Mind*. Its product we call *Science;* and as science measures itself, its history is all one *progress* though men and nations fail. What last meaning "progress" has, might be hard to tell; but considering what ambitions mechanism may obstruct, one measure of science-progress is oftenest proposed. It is the measure of reduction science

is able to effect in mechanism's dead re-
sistance to a common human will. If as our
sketch developed—that sketch of man's long
journey from the scene in the dark forest to
the mouth of the bright river—we asked ourselves what magic so transformed the landscape, our poet by way of answer invokes a
growing Science: a science that comes to control the mechanism of things—

"When man first wandered in the dark
forests he was nature's serf; he offered
tribute and prayer to the winds, and the lightning, and the rain, to the cave-lion, which
seized his burrow for its lair, to the mam-
moth, which devoured his scanty crops. But
as time passed on, he ventured to rebel; he
made stone his servant; he discovered fire
and vegetable poison; he domesticated iron;
he slew the wild beasts or subdued them;
he made them feed him and give him clothes.
He became a chief surrounded by his slaves;
the fire lay beside him with dull red eye and
yellow tongue waiting his instructions to
prepare his dinner, or to make him poison,
or to go with him to the war, and fly on the
houses of the enemy, hissing, roaring, and

consuming all. The trees of the forest were his flock, he slaughtered them at his convenience; the earth brought forth at his command. He struck iron upon wood or stone and hewed out the fancies of his brain; he plucked shells, and flowers, and the bright red berries, and twined them in his hair; he cut the pebble to a sparkling gem, he made the dull clay a transparent stone. The river which once he had worshiped as a god or which he had vainly attacked with sword and spear, he now conquered to his will. He made the winds grind his corn and carry him across the waters; he made the stars serve him as a guide. He obtained from salt and wood and sulphur a destroying force. He drew from fire, and water, the awful power which produces the volcano, and made it do the work of human hands. He made the sun paint his portraits, and gave the lightning a situation in the post-office." (511, f.)

Of course there is more than mechanism science needs to conquer ere martyrdom shall cease,—and of all that in a moment. But let me first conclude this triumphant hymn to Intellect, even though to do so we must follow our poet out beyond the Present and sing our song to the Future. Here history can still guide us, if only by projecting its truth into what verisimilitude we may lend our invented tale.

We have seen, our poet reminds us, how "by means of his inventions and discoveries, by means of the arts and trades, and by means of the industry resulting from them, Man has raised himself from the condition of a serf to the condition of a lord. His triumph, indeed, is incomplete; his kingdom is not yet come. The Prince of Darkness is still triumphant in many regions of the world; epidemics still rage, death is yet victorious. But the God of Light, the Spirit of Knowledge, the Divine Intellect is gradually spreading over the planet and upwards to the skies. Earth, which is now a purgatory, will be made a paradise, not by idle prayers and supplications, but by the efforts of man himself, and by means of mental achievements analogous to those which have raised him to his present state. Those inventions and discoveries which have made him, by the grace of God, king of the animals, lord of the

elements, and sovereign of steam and elec-
tricity, were all of them founded on experiment and observation. We can conquer nature only by obeying her laws, and in order
to obey her laws we must first learn what
they are. When we have ascertained, by
means of Science, the method of nature's
operations, we shall be able to take her place
and to perform them for ourselves." (512)

Nor can we set aside as idle (unless all
large thought for the future is idle in brief
lives) a poet's dream of the seventies which
by the nineteen-twenties has become much
less a dream. What science might yet do in
taking Nature's place was no mere misty
blur in this thinker's prevision. An Englishman, his thought turns for its illustration to
Nature's poor hospitality to her English sons;
but what science might come to England's
help would come to the help of all. And
three inventions Reade thinks would give to
his crowded island the same prosperous conditions we of the States enjoy (no thanks to
our political wisdom, but to the fatness of
our land). Of these three inventions "which
perhaps may be long delayed, but which pos-

sibly are near at hand . . . the first is the discovery of a motive force which will take the place of steam, with its cumbrous fuel of oil or coal; secondly, the invention of aerial locomotion which will transport labor at a trifling cost of money and of time to any part of the planet, and which, by anni-hilating distance, will speedily extinguish national distinctions; and, thirdly, the manu-facture of flesh and flour from the elements by a chemical process in the laboratory, simi-lar to that which is now performed within the bodies of the animals and plants. Food will then be manufactured in unlimited quanti-ties at a trifling expense; and our enlightened posterity will look back upon us who eat oxen and sheep just as we look back upon canni-bals. Hunger and starvation will then be unknown, and the best part of the human life will no longer be wasted in the tedious process of cultivating the fields. Population will mightily increase, and the earth will be a garden." (513)

Sources of energy other than fuel, trans-portation swifter than rail, the synthetic pro-duction of organic effects,—these are no

longer the dreams they were but fifty years
ago. And if for all that the earth is no
nearer a garden, perhaps it is because a real
Eden is something more than a scene. What
if every prospect pleases, do man continue
vile! . . . But that is Reade's own story, to
be left for him to tell.

I like those "Grenzbegriffe," those limiting conceptions which if they outstrip our
knowing do but reveal the plainer what is
working in the soul. As no more than such
a conception, meant for no more indeed, I
offer Reade's last picture of the earth become
a garden, and of man's life thereon. "Men
will [then] look upon this star as their
fatherland; its progress will be their ambi-
tion; the gratitude of others their reward.
These bodies which now we wear, belong to
the lower animals; our minds have already
outgrown them; already we look upon them
with contempt. A time will come when
Science will transform them by means which
we cannot conjecture, and which, even if explained to us, we could not now understand,
just as the savage cannot understand elec-

tricity, magnetism, steam. Disease will be
extirpated; the causes of decay will be re-
moved; immortality will be invented.

"And then, the earth being small, mankind
will migrate into space, and will cross the
airless Saharas which separate planet from
planet, and sun from sun. The earth will
become a Holy Land which will be visited
by pilgrims from all the quarters of the universe. Finally, men will master the forces
of nature; they will become themselves archi-
tects of systems, manufacturers of worlds.
Man then will be perfect; he will then be a
creator; he will therefore be what the vulgar
worship as a god. There is but a difference
in degree between the chemist who to-day arranges forces in his laboratory so that they
produce a gas, and the creator who arranges
forces so that they produce a world; between
the gardener who plants a seed, and the
creator who plants a nebula." (515)

And then we come back to earth.

And when we come back to earth we find
many things have happened since 1875 to
make us wonder whether science (of the kind

whose song of triumph we have just lost our
ears to) be not a singular blessing, at times
much like a curse. Instead of turning "Dark
Forests" into laughing gardens, it has stained
bright fields of poppies with something
redder than they. Where then is that "*other*
progress*" for which we have been waiting,
without which technical science can only mend
the weapons of an enduring will to kill?

I know not how others may find it, but
here my author's vision of what the Mind
may do, lacks to my understanding the intellectual penetration it never needed more.
And thinking on the reason for its unconvinc-
ing tone I have rather come to find the root of
its offending in a very common fault. Like
most who deal in futures waiting for their
outcome on man's willing this or that, our
author seems to think the forces driving wills
spring from some other organ than the thinking "head." We have a way of saying, Man
can grow no better without a "change of
heart." Such figurative phrases help one
very little, save to point the lesson that
Mind has far to go ere Man will make his

morals a matter of the "head." Heir to
old "expedients" (rightly said by our historian to have served well in their day) he
clings to "eternal truths" and imbeds them
in his heart; which amounts to saying, he
gives his head a rest by taking all for
"holy" when sufficiently outworn. And then
in time he pays the sacrificial price.

Winwood Reade, to be sure, misses none
of this; but when it comes to asking, What
is to be done? I turn his pages fruitlessly to
find an answer save, Hope on—and wait!
Meanwhile, he paints pictures not without
their charm:

"A day will come when mankind will be
as the Family of the Forest, which lived
faithfully within itself according to the
golden rule in order that it might not die.
But Love not Fear will unite the human
race. The world will have become a
heavenly Commune to which men will bring
the inmost treasures of their hearts, in which
they will reserve for themselves not even a
hope, not even the shadow of a joy, but will
give up all for all mankind. With one faith,
with one desire they will labor together in

the Sacred Cause—the extinction of disease, the extinction of sin, the perfection of genius, the perfection of love, the invention of immortality, the exploration of the infinite, the conquest of creation." (538)

Perhaps; perhaps; perhaps! but what would you suggest in the way of a first step toward this blessed culmination in which men "will reserve for themselves not even the shadow of a joy, but will give up all for all mankind?"

It sometimes seems to me the best way of beginning would be by giving up *the ideal of "giving up."*

When I began this pleasant ramble through two Universal Histories, I remember having said I would set them end to end, then let them make their own unspoiled impression. But now that I have done, or very nearly so, I find the impression baffling —to myself.

There is, one sees, a contrast:

"Cultures" ever rising and dying down again tell no continuous story, none at least with point. But no one can suppose their

learned story-teller to deny to later episodes
science beyond the first. Spengler more than
another is competent to tell the tremendous
cumulation of "science" with the years: culture follows culture to the same undoing,
indeed; but the mechanism of this undoing
is never twice the same. One sort of con-
tinuity not even he would refuse to those
culture-lives of which ours, fast dying, is
last. But persuade himself he cannot that a
progressive science in killing is a way of
learning to live.

And Reade, if he tells us of one surviving
life, learning by experiment to put on immortality, what has he really to build on,
save that *technical science grows?* This may
give life much it could not command of old,
it may change the span of existence by pre-
venting and curing disease. (All this Con-
dorcet had said nigh a century before our
Reade.) But that most fatal disorder which
makes men kill each other has grown but
more fatal, thanks to the lethal gifts science
has armed it with. What can science do to
cure this disaster? Wait, says Reade, and
hope. The heart will learn to love, to love

till it reserve no shadow of a joy it will not yield.

Now had I been Winwood Reade, or even Oswald Spengler, I should have been tempted to ask whether there were no science whose problem it was to show how this passion for yielding was a thing to be overcome. Overcome? That is to say outlived, the reason for it conquered.

More vital to man's progress toward the happiness of mortals than even synthetic food is, must be the accurate measure of what men gain by *Grouping*. Who writes Kultur writes Group with an exceedingly capital letter. And who writes *one* writes *two Groups*, swords sharpened for each other. To Groups, to Kulturen, loyalties of all sorts have pledged sacrifices unnumbered, necessary to a day when no cost of hanging together could exceed the price of suffering separatim. The tradition of those days lingers in our being; the "principles" of those days having left the "head" are sunk into the "heart." They raise to a religion the "giving up for all." And then they call this "loving"!   Love does not give up; love knows no "obligations."

No more need that science which thinking over adjustment of human will to will writes "coöperation of heads" for the old "subjection of heart.". . .

"Groups," it would say, "Kulturen, may be of those expedients the past did well to try.   They bound men together against a common foe, and as long as that foe threatens men do well to 'stick.'   But what if this very bondage were the *making* of foe for foe?   Kulturen may be least tragic to the being they enslave at the moment of their passing.   There is hope for the Western World when man's martyrdom to Groups shall end in his taking thought on each man's worth to each."

KING OF PARIS

To Extramural Students, Wilkes-Barre

KING OF PARIS

On a night of May last, a world wrapped in slumber was bereft of a little multitude of its most useful sons. I recall a distinguished physician, a jurist of eminent learning, scientists and scholars—a college professor of parts. That the world till this moment rests unknowing of its losses, is due to circumstances I hasten to relate.

For, deep in the night in question (the world left to silence) I took pad and pencil for a certain calculation long weighing on my soul. It proved to be a problem of no lofty mathematics, but in the end my awe-struck spirit touched the heights of high finance. Or so it seemed to me.

From motives within the sympathy of every careful parent, I felt it time to figure exactly what it cost these days to turn out a physician,—a thoroughly trained physician. (Accidental, that my thought should first have turned to physic; but the tragedy of

the sequel could not have been averted by
happier beginning,—as time will show.)
How much it cost, then, to produce the
trained physician? Nothing easier to gather
than data for this problem, nothing simpler
to tote up than a modest column of figures.
But that immodest total! *That* is the staggering issue, *that* the fatal outcome of this
simple sum in adding.

For all the explicit catalogues of our first-
class universities lead to one conclusion: To
bring our medical offspring to the dreamt-of
moment when a brand new shingle may
flaunt the family name, costs if all go well
some twenty-seven years of lifetime, with
university training to the tune of two thousand or so. There may be other items:
books, instruments, incidentals—my curi-
osity went not so far. Essential, is this picture of our child of seven and twenty hanging out his shingle, unsurpassed in background, redolent of paint. But they tell
me, who understand these things, that a
really able fellow at not much more than
thirty may come to relieve his family of
some portion of his costs; that is, of course,

provided he have not indulged in follies, such as wife and children and setting up a house.

Need I drag you deeper, O Sympathetic Public, into the tragic causes of that May disaster? In these troubled waters our young physician perished, beaten with the fury of Higher Education. Thus at the age of seven his spirit passed untimely, yet none too soon. From this world he was followed in the turning of a leaf by a sad cortège of promising young lives: jurist, scholar, scientific pundit. . . . And I believe I mentioned one who looked forward after endless study to teaching other fellows the Higher Education. He perished too—but all unmourned.

That May night passed. When the morning sun lit the scattered wreckage of so much foundered hope, it touched one upturned visage not altogether gone. 'Twas that of a poet, a brand new poet. These poets being born, not made by man's instruction, I suspect the place will fairly teem with them ere long. Or else revert to desert, for no humble talent waiting on tuition can long survive the struggle for Higher Education, unless . . .

But that is another poet's story I may tell of after while.

And the world slept through its losses: as worlds will if you let them. I alone seemed wakeful, and the thought occurred to me (philosopher, and therefore more practical than most)—If such affairs are common, if such disasters frequent (and what's to make them rare in the story of our day?), must not this world awaken to a painful sense of want?

Take one such want suggested by the demise of physicians (in potentia, it may be, but essential for all that)—take want of health and healing!

How escape the conclusion that if medical education continue in its present prohibitive demands, the medicine of the future must be trusted to the keeping of the fairly well-to-do? Now of course there is no reason for supposing all the offspring of well-conditioned parents to be idle loafers, incompetents, and fools. But neither is it patent the brains of the republic are reserved for the furnishings of children of ease. And in this vital matter (the world's healthy being) what policy can promise acceptable returns, save one that insists from the very outset on removing every obstacle to accomplishment of brain? Obstacle? Is not the task of science itself of a sternness to exclude from its service all but the most fit?

But granted all the *quality* of minds come into being with silver spoons adjusted to their mouths, what of the *quantity* of such well-provided youth? If they come in no such plenty as to make wide distribution a condition of their finding the wherewithal to work, think you voluntarily they will forsake the crowded centers where, vying with and heartening their own productive kind, they urge each other on to science and new arts? Once in a while it may be some Christ-like soul among them, more touched by present suffering than prospect of advance, might betake him to places where need was most crying, fill his days with healing, snatch at scraps of science in his journal tired nights.

Meanwhile, what must happen in those remote places which the training of trained men would teach them to avoid? Does one stand by helpless and watch a friend go

sicken, and suffer, and decline? Or is it not
in nature to rush out for succor, to claim
what service offers from any human being
supposed to know a little of the ways of life
and death? Must not then the quack, the
new-school and empiric, the practitioner of
strange practices come to fill the land?

"Do you say then, Let's go backward?" I
fancy some would ask me, as the ills of costly
training fill my speech.

I am far from despising the schooling of
our fathers, when men of first-rate standing
taught youth of first-rate mind the soundest
sort of practice known to any; yet built upon
less learning, less general cultivation than has
come to be required since their day. Shall
we deny to the combination, intelligence plus
training, the tribute of the science it has
made? though it made it as it went to the
bedside of the patient whence it brought away
new science in its thought.

But I know as well as any there is no sense
in retrogression; those who pushed us on-
ward would expect us to push on. To-day, a
world of practice with no time, equipment,
training for that patient, unremunerative toil

by which laboratory science does its quota, drives its labor in the depths—such a busy world of practice would no doubt be something: our children could not thank us for the *best*.   Now, that investigating science of the laboratory worker is a science to which all science is akin: can we wonder if our standards of medical education grow higher and always higher as we go?   Education, to be sure, however it be given, however thoughtful, elaborate, prolonged, makes not the least pretension to an art no art possesses—it produces no great creative mind. But when this mind comes sauntering along the ways of fate shall we have nothing ready for its hand?   Shall we ask it to make science, but before beginning science to make the tools without which science is not made? But the man of higher learning, the well-equipped research-man, is maker of the tools even genius can't forego.   This man of higher learning, this supreme technician (no harder way of life than his, no way less resplendent, can ask a man to take it for his own)—what of his means of living while he learns?

What of the higher learning? The forti-
tude to brave it, the ability to gain it are so
rare! Shall we wait for luck to bring them
both in happy-go-lucky conjunction with a
certain elongated private purse? For the loss
of every intellect of which need robs our
science, who think you is the loser in the end?
'Tis you, 'tis I, 'tis every one that lives. All
living hangs on science for its life.

We depend, I say, on science for our lives.
On science? On what science? would you
say: for though the "healing science" is our
first suggestion, it cannot on reflection be our
last.

The ignorant peasant whom the knife of
the surgeon has miraculously turned from
pain to peace, will no doubt consider that
when it comes to thanking he has the surgeon's hand alone to bless. But you, the
thoughtful, with history before you, will
see the surgeon's hand as older than his years.
From the point of his lancet, as from a
charged electrode leaps the cumulated science
of all time. By what hard obscure lives has

this learning been collected; in what laboratories; in what closets where mathematicians brood! These men had somehow to learn and live for learning; they healed none, yet without them none were healed. If our peasant did but know it, when it comes to thanking he has not alone the surgeon's hand to bless.

When you come to think on my question, What of the higher learning? there is this thing it were well to keep in mind. You depend on it for life; it depends on you for living; but beyond that, mutuality grows obscure. Beware above all things of limiting your giving to such science as yields immediate returns; that much is nothing and would come to nothing but for all the other work you do not see. As well might one say: I'll endow the hand of Raphael but not the head of Raphael; he paints me no madonnas with his head.

When I ask then, What of learning? What of the higher learning? I mean, What of science? the purest and most ultimate, the science least related to any present need.

It is on *all* science we are dependent for our lives. For our lives? But for *what* of our lives? So little of our lives is just their living!

There are economic burdens can so oppress the soul, the mightiest frame may put its strength into one last blasphemy of despair. These ills are curable and they cry for cure; but how should they be mended without taking thought? And is adjustment of human elements within the social body a matter to be thought out overnight? Economics, social science, are very youthful studies; but they are not therefore games for untrained minds. Their study needs a learning of the very highest order if it is to find a way of letting man endure man. But let not those who would consider the helping of these studies hope to enjoy the fruits thereof themselves. Only for our children or our children's children may those fruits be sweeter than any we do eat: bitter fruit of ages of unreflective action, whose self-absolving counsel took the form of *laissez-faire*.

When I ask then, *What* of life is dependent on our science? I find no truer answer than, It must be nearly all. And the part of higher learning essential to all science, is thus made essential to every part of life.

What are we to do, then, to give to higher learning the freest chance to live and to learn?

Once a playwright, looking for a song, found it on one tongue and gave it to another: "If I were King of Paris" . . . you remember the refrain? No matter where he found it, the one to whom he gave it was François called Villon, Master of Arts. The thing is so fitting I cannot help regretting that François, rogue and poet, let the chance escape him to write the song himself. Who put words to sighs, depths to regret, edge to human terrors—I should have been glad to owe him this one line more. "If I were King of Paris"—no other line I know of expresses just as this one the cheerful incredulity, the disillusioned hopefulness we all live on at times.

Or am I wrong, and are there in the world those who never play at being King? Can an irony have brought me (me unworthy)

to address a congregation of the utterly
sagacious? Knowing dreams to be of such
stuff as dreams are made on, do you of your
wisdom leave such sorry stuff to fools? Are
there none here who remember of an early
summer-morning, stepping from their door-
ways ere the world had turned to toil, to
have felt it would take little—just the slight-
est touch of magic—to spread this morning
freshness through the day? Are there none
who in the stillness of the night, have imagined half the weariness in which their fellows
slumbered (and to which they must awaken
with the day) to be some human blunder,
some want of understanding, of which not
reason truly but a dreamy King of Paris
might manage to rid them while they slept?

But I am jesting, no real fear is on me
that I face a Sanhedrim of too judicial
beards. For is not the occasion one on which
you welcome the end and fruition of several
years of toil? And who has studied much,
or who has learnt at all who has not learned
exceedingly to dream? And so I am not
afraid, but venture to avow, to publish and
discuss with you certain little plans of mine

looking toward a jollier world when I am
King.

Now the first of my reforms *makes the
higher learning free!*

The second—but the second and the rest
may be left to the time and counsel of a race
to whom all learning *has been made free.*

On the first though I am determined; and
the higher the higher learning the freer it
shall be!

With which pronouncement, I might let
fulfillment wait on time and the event, but
for the philosophic habit so unroyal yet not
ungenial of meeting objections ere they are
voiced.

And these objections (O pectora cæca!)—
can't one hear them coming from afar! That
day when I the Sovereign told my loving
people of the care I had at heart for their
worst care, can you not imagine what interest would be taken in the question how
My Majesty proposed to meet the bills?

I should of course point out to them, mine
was no poor republic, but one of the richest
the whole fat land could show. "What! [I
should urge them] from my palace on a

hill, from a throne of price, surrounded by all that art can give, I may look from my windows on a land filled to bursting, on a nature inexhaustible in wealth—and yet must consider whether I can afford me the learning of a handful of men?"

"But, Sir [dutiful, insistent], whence come the monies with which your ample coffers overflow?"

"Why, where but from your pockets, my masters [I should answer]; but where this pittance came from, is there any lack of more? I cannot conceive then you would seriously begrudge me means for the training of a few outstanding minds. Means— minds! What is the difference? What is science but a mastery of means? Yes, there is this difference: your wealth can buy the market; can it put upon the market what things wealth no more than poverty can buy? Health, peace, contentment in ever-growing freedom; can your wealth buy you these things if mind find not the way?"

"But all that, Sir, we *do* somehow come by [you know the prudent answer] without an investment of our own. The scientific fellow

just can't help working—for his winnings we
and he may trust to luck. Now your palaces
and fine-arts, your royal roads and bridges,
these things we grudge you not at all. Your
gaols and policemen, your judges and at-
torneys, stout men to help our children creep
unwillingly to school—in these we would not
stint you; they are for the delectation, for the
safety and salvation of us all. But in this
way of learning, while we understand that
many, very many, may be called, there are
precious few elected to touch its higher
reaches. Why should we, the many, give our
substance for so few?"

Ah, yes! here we have it: the world-old
cry of justice, outraged by the taxing of the
many for the few. And here as always the
fact of this injustice seems patent, demonstrable, mathematically plain: if the teaching of the many is the burden of the many,
must not an instruction by which so few may
profit be entered to the debit of the profit-
sharing few?

That is the question: is there danger we
should whisper everybody's secret if we gave
ourselves the trouble to think the matter out?

The teaching of the many is for the many's welfare: the instruction of your "higher men" can touch but very few!

Most men take kindly to this logic: but not all! I remember one who did not. This was a gentle tory of my friends, whose love of education had I fear been sadly blighted by over-education, over-culture, over-art. Can you imagine a being of this day and generation with a frank, avowed contempt for public schools, for that blessing of all blessings—universal education, which either goes to class or goes to gaol?

Yet such was he! I recall one occasion when some new outbreak of wisdom from the ranks (so he thought) of this polloi stung him to an outburst whose absurdity was touching: If the State (said he) must squander some surplus of its plunder on the teaching of those who cannot pay, it would do less folly did it free the top of learning to those proved competent to climb, than in forcing grubby rudiments, themselves not worth the digging, on those not fit to use them when they're dug.

All this is most wrong-headed; cynicism

of a thinker who had thought himself beyond the reach of most. Such loneliness of kind would rather seek its fellow in a world all untaught and all unspoiled than in the confused thinking and more confusing bearing of "minds debauched with learning [of not much]." No longer simple nor yet become as gentle, such minds leave something to regret. My tory had forgotten (pretended he'd forgotten) that progress of humanity at large is a necessary rumpus not meant for the soothing of solitary scholars, fastidious of taste. Yet out of his much nonsense comes a grain of what may well be—sense, or something like it. When I compare the ease with which men bear the burden of a trivial education of the crowd, with their vociferous reluctance to be taxed in any measure to complete the education of the few, I remember my old tory and am seized with the fancy his madness may not have been so altogether mad.

I wonder! The beneficent effect of universal education, I accept at the hands of wiser men than I: but accept it as a thesis experience may have proven—no principle convincing of itself. I am not blind to dangers; least of all to dangers men comfortably leave to the remedy of time. Rare is that vintage whose own working leaves it wholesome; the vintner can ill trust to a lazy *laissez-faire*.

By way of illustration and matter for reflection: Millet's melancholy painting "The Man with the Hoe." I say melancholy, for it is so—to you and to me. To us who look upon it with a wealth of world-experience in the background of our eye, it brings the sort of vision Edwin Markham catches— this Man, as

> Bowed by weight of centuries he leans
> Upon his hoe and gazes on the ground,
> The emptiness of ages on his face,
> And on his back the burden of the world.

So he is, so he stands! the Man with the Hoe. But so he is for you and me, so he stands for those who know. For himself he stands not so; he, the only one in all this company *who does not know*. Still for you he stands so; you are moved to pity, and "What [you cry] can we do for him, to

mend his broken life?" A universal chorus
answers, "Teach!"

Teach? Teach him? Teach him *what?*
Enough for him to see himself somewhat as
we see him? (Only somewhat as we see him
—not altogether so. No master teacher could
be found to penetrate that brow with even so
much learning.) No, but teach him *something;* force a little learning on him, just
enough (say) ere we leave him to himself, to
let him spell the question whose full import
fills the poet in the next accusing lines:

> Who made him dead to rapture and despair,
> A thing that grieves not and that never hopes,
> Stolid, stunned, a brother to the ox?
> Who loosened and let down that brutal jaw?
> Whose was the hand that slanted back this
>   brow?
> Whose breath blew out the light within this
>   brain?

Ah, if we can but teach him the meaning of
that question, our Fellow with the Hoe, no
longer will there be "a thing that grieves
not and that never hopes." He will have
learned to grieve.

And how shall he learn to hope, if you

would have him hope? Can you teach him
that? Can you teach *him* to think, to think
that out? 'Tis not likely: more likely, he
will turn an eye of supplication to those of
higher learning than he can learn to dream
of, and cry to them to think him through his
life. And if we know no way, if we neither
study nor help those who would to study such
a way—how think you the last verses of that
accusing poem will fall on our careless ears,
some day?—

> O masters, lords and rulers of all lands,
> Is this the handiwork you give to God,
> This monstrous thing distorted and soul-
> quenched?
> How will you ever straighten up this shape;
> Touch it again with immortality;
> Give back the upward looking and the light;
> Rebuild in it the music and the dream;
> Make right the immemorial infamies,
> Perfidious wrongs, immedicable woes?
>
> O masters, lords and rulers in all lands,
> How will the future reckon with this Man?
> How answer his brute question in that hour
> When whirlwinds of rebellion shake the
> world?

How will it be with kingdoms and with
  kings—
With those who shaped him to the thing he
  is—
When this dumb terror shall reply to God,
After the silence of the centuries?

The philosopher has spoken and has plead.
The King of Paris mounts at last his throne:
"My subjects, this Man of burdens and of
woes you bade me educate. 'Tis done! He
has now a little learning; he has learned to
grieve; no longer does he lean upon his hoe.
This I have done for all of *you,* now let me
think of you and *me.* You have not asked
yourselves (but I have), How will it be with
kingdoms in that day? How will it be with
kingdoms and with you, when this dark being
we have taught to grieve shall ask of us to
teach him hope? Shall we answer, Back to
school? There, shall he learn to prattle
volubly of capital and labor, learn to speak
of masses and the privilege of classes, learn
to be eloquent on all our present ills? Is that
the answer? Do you know it; can you guess
it; O ye average men? No? No more
can I.

"Then let me spend a fraction of the wealth you provide me on the training and the thinking of the more-than-average mind. 'Will it pay?' I cannot promise, but of this I am assured: if it pay not, then there's nothing else that will.

"And so I ask the many (the fathers of so many) to let me spend their substance on the training of a few. A few? Among the few may be one who shall be able to see in more than visions the real road to hope. Is not one sufficient? It does not need an army to capture an *Idea*. But it does need the learning and the sanity of science—it needs all the *chances* that a higher learning gives.

"That is it: let us gamble; let us gamble with the future (whether or not we want to, there is nothing else to do). But like scientific gamblers let us calculate the chances, take the chances in our favor,—*make the higher learning free!*"

A PARABLE

On the Occasion of Dedicating the Barnes Foundation

A PARABLE

There is nothing humanity craves more than it craves beauty. Since this is so, how should we not wonder why in the long history of his works man has afforded himself so little of what he most loves?

Revolving these things, I was once tempted to put the gist of my speculation into a proverb, which as it is lacking in all wit must be bursting with wisdom.

A man, I wrote, athirst, would be no worse off in a desert, than possessed of a cask of the best yet wanting means to induce it to flow, and without a sound bowl to receive it.

However little this proverb may enlighten, at least it cannot deceive. Every one will have guessed my cask to contain the spirit of art. All will know that to make this flow a patron's touch is needed. And if the bowl is a puzzling bit, let me return to that later: it is too much at once to ask of a saw more than two-thirds of a meaning.

I would say a word first of this spirit of art, or rather, how to increase it.

On the ways of making an artist there is little wise to be uttered. The poet who wrote

> Tell me where is fancy bred,
> Or in the heart or in the head?
> How begot, how nourished?

might have strung his *ors* and *hows* across the page, he would have asked us nothing the harder. Where, how, of what nativity, encouragement, recognition, art's fancy is bred, who can tell? The best religious poets of our day, Paul Verlaine, Francis Thompson, caught their vision of heaven, lying in the gutter. Yet others have lain in the gutter, and nothing noble came of it. Why one can bring from the depths a new hymn, another but the reek of ancient filth . . . ? But though we know so little of the whence and how of art, that is no reason we should let what comes of it go unsought and unsolicited. Which brings me to the second figure of my parable, art's patron.

It is no more the business of the artist

than of his fellow-culprit, the philosopher,
to make a living; yet it has come generally
to be conceded that both somehow must be
allowed to live.   There is only one chance
this economic problem can be solved, that is
the chance of there turning up somewhere in
the world a class of beings for whom the
luxuries these brother-fools purvey are somehow more necessary than necessity itself.   In
a sense we are all of this class.   The poor
balance left after keeping soul and body together awhile we are glad to pool to make
of that soul something worth the keeping.
There is no more sincere and no more generous patron of art than the "general public,"
which is to say, all mankind.

But as a solicitor and inciter of art, we the
public have our limitations.   If the best collective taste of to-day has caught up with
the best individual insight of day-before-yes-
terday, we may congratulate our public on
its unusual enlightenment.   Consequently,
public patronage devotes its modest resources
to the encouragement of artists beyond the
reach as beyond need of that support they
so lacked when it was needed.

Little hope from this meager retrospective patronage for the spirit, whether of science or of art, that still owns a body. Least of all if that spirit be one of adventure. And never was the like of this day for great adventures. Around you are some the painter has hazarded; but he who thinks the brush has swept all audacities into the painter's corner, cannot yet have heard the musician; he whom the musician amazes, must somehow have escaped the poet. Nay, if any suppose this restlessness to be but a madness of art, let him come with me to sit at the feet of science, and preferably the mathematician's science. And then of course there is always the quiet philosopher.

Alas for these brave new things. Some, like Dædalus, may win to permanent shores. More, like Icarus, flying too high must melt their wings and fall. Yet, if there is any wisdom in a myth, it may be well to remember Dædalus brought an experienced science and craftsmanship, Icarus but a daring levity to the *novas artes* and their use.

Meanwhile, second only to those who risk their lives for art and science I count those who give their means that an issue of right and wrong, of truth and error, may not be left to the arbitrament of average insight, to the judgment of collective patronage. With which plain sentiment I have meant to pay in more than eloquence, namely, in the recognition of sound sportsmanship, my tribute to the private patron who keeps his courage with him.

I come at last to the third figure of my parable, the uninterpreted receiver. Do you know? I meant that bowl at the outset to stand for you and me, in whom art's vintage is ultimately caught and held. But alas there are so many and such important differences between bowls and souls. Absurd to point out that a bowl is finished when finished; a soul is in the making till judgment day at least. A bowl is none the viler for what it may hold of the vile, none the nobler for the most precious that can be poured into it; a soul is pot or amphora, as its contents make it. A bowl does nothing but simply is; a soul is only what it does.

If it is childish thus to enumerate some

distinctions that mark a bowl from a soul, what shall we say of historic practices only to be brought within reason by the assumption that so far as reception of art is concerned a soul is a bowl and nothing more! How many amateurs have with princely gesture thrown their priceless gatherings to the public at last! Of course a man with eyes to see must see, must he not? as a bowl with capacity to hold must hold. And yet all know this is not so. The real giver of a work of art must give twice or not at all. With one hand he may offer a picture to the eye; he has done nothing till with the other he offer an eye to the picture. And that eye to be worthy of a picture, worthy such an eye, must itself be artist and creator.

Those who dwell in the grandeur of the Alps are said to be sensible only of the warmth of hearths and the comfort of food. The Alps are not big enough to make *themselves* impressive. Nothing is.

There is the story of an artist who, passing the stinking carcass of a dog, stopped, caught by the beauty of those dazzling teeth. A dead dog is not hideous enough to make *itself* repulsive. Nothing is.

It is not hard to catch the spirit of a certain dream: To bring works of art to the enjoyment of souls made competent to enjoy them. To use the experience of all humanity in the cultivation of an eye fit to judge a work of art. To bring then great universities to bear upon the preparation of that other creative soul, without whom the greatest artist can create nothing. The dream is generous; I might say, it is beautiful; I prefer to end on another word—this dream is to the last degree intelligent.

The dream is intelligent, therefore it is hard to realize. I have paid tribute to the sportsmanship of the amateur who gives to new arts their chance. I may add, as one of the slow plodders along hard teacher's ways, the promise of the coöperation of all who walk those ways. None know better than they the poet's truth: All things worth while are as difficult as they are rare.

George Stuart Fullerton

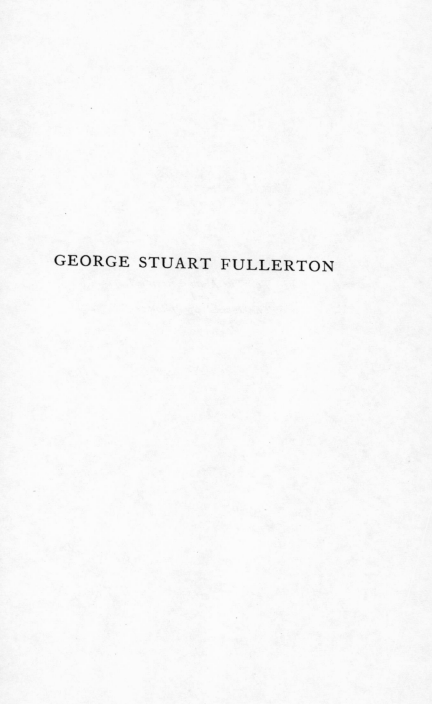

GEORGE STUART FULLERTON

To "The Alumni Register"
and
"The Journal of Philosophy"

GEORGE STUART FULLERTON

If I have been asked to write of Fullerton
at this time, it is, of course, because as his
pupil in the early nineties—and in the late,
a young instructor under his tutelage and
direction—I may be supposed to have kept
memories of those days. That these should
be affectionate, all who knew Fullerton
would take for granted; that they would be
willingly, if sadly, recalled at his asking, the
editor of this JOURNAL might well assume.

Only, the form in which these notes are
here laid before the readers of the JOURNAL
is not as untouched by chance and accident
as I would willingly have had it; for it so
happened that the moment at which they
were asked for nearly coincided with the appearance in the Alumni Register (Pennsylvania) of what had been written in like sense
and intention. No man can find "other
words" for the same sincere feeling, however
conscious that had he addressed his first to
another company they must have taken other

form. I can only hope, if I am to go on, that it will not be too distasteful to you to be forced to overhear (as it may seem) the echo of a voice speaking within its family-circle. But if here at the outset I reproduce this former note, it is not without a sense that the very qualities it owes to accident may serve better than any I might more thoughtfully have devised to lend light and color to what reflections I would offer the philosopher ere I close.

It was (I could well say to my fellow-alumni) out of darkness of mood and dimness of knowledge I chose to write of brighter things and closer ties.

What were the days, how golden the hours spent with the Fullerton of other years, men of those years will not have forgotten. In their hearts they carry an image which the somber end of his story will make them hold the closer. The ultimate sadness of a thoughtful man leaves us all most thoughtful. We wonder how much of the illumination he cast was at his own cost of lightness. We wonder, and are silent.

But of that illumination we are certain. It was a gay learning we learned of Fullerton, though it had to do with depths few teachers dare sound. Cool analytic thinking, too conscientious with the thinker's conscience to shun the dangerous or avoid the dry; how should this not spoil the day for minds still warm and unformed, not yet thoughtful, of a courage untried? Such thinking might have taken the light out of our sky: if it did not, if on the contrary it so sunned things as to make its hour an hour to be waited for, must not Fullerton have owned some teacher's secret any teacher would sell his soul to share?

Aye, but that I fear is the only way any might come by Fullerton's secret of teaching; something like that I have come to think is the price at which he himself had it. How could we guess this wit playing about arid places to make them blossom for us, this humor lightening serious things, to be a costly purchase? Later, perhaps, having wandered along ways where thought and laughter were seldom met with together, we who remembered may have come to reflect. If elsewhere we found these qualities combined only in those who had been to school to pain, we who remembered may well have come to reflect.

"Conception of the Infinite, and Solution of the Mathematical Antinomies: A Study in Psychological Analysis." What a title, what a book to put in the hands of youngsters just out of their *Barbara celarent darii ferio*que prioris! And this but as preparation for a second work to follow: "A Plain Argument for God"! ("Plain," it may be; not conventional, surely.)

As for the former of these volumes, it was a delight. Rather was it a hard matter made delightful. But if such as are not of the fortunate nineties would know in what its wise humor lay, let me quote a few lines of the Preface. They may suggest why even more than Fullerton, the man, Fullerton, a manner of thinking, will remain with his students always . . .

"To be told that of two impossible things one must be true; that of the same two lines one may be looked upon as equal to, less than, or greater than the other; that Achilles, running rapidly, can never overtake the tortoise, moving slowly; to be told all this seriously is well calculated to bring not merely suspicion but contempt on speculative thought. Who has not puzzled, on his first introduction to Logic, over some of these antinomies, and been silenced unconvinced by the practical demonstration, which cuts the knot but does not solve it, leaving in the mind a disagreeable sense that the argument must be wrong somewhere, yet a consciousness that it seems perfectly sound.

"When the metaphysician proves to us that a rhinoceros is a mosquito, his chain of reasoning is rendered innocuous by the striking incongruity of the conclusion; but if we observe no flaw in the reasoning, we cannot help recognizing the perplexing truth that it is the experienced fact alone which has prevented assent, and that a precisely similar argument, *the conclusion of which cannot be similarly tested*, may yet induce assent, though equally erroneous.

"If we have no better reason for rejecting an argument, *what can be our criterion when we leave the sphere of the immediately palpable?"* (Condensed.)

This is Fullerton in essence: no problem of inference can be dry for him nor for any who sit under him. Its topic may be remote from, its conclusion contradictory to, all experience: it is none the less *a test of reasoning*. And as reason is all that can help us reach for what lies beyond our immediate grasp, to be able to catch its errors before the event convict it, is a faculty precious beyond whatever other learning. Only, Fullerton, the teacher, would never have wasted a moment preaching so sounding a sermon in so many solemn words. Rather, before the end of that moment you would have found yourself chasing Achilles who was chasing the tortoise, and with perfect gayety of heart you would so have endured till you had caught, not the elusive tortoise, but the more elusive fallacy Zeno of Elea set rolling, over two thousand years ago. It is true, those who ran this course in the eighties and nineties may never again have found themselves called to overtake a tortoise; but of the many days gone since then, hardly one can have let them rest from the task of catching false reasons. Meanwhile, back in these eighties and nineties you had laughed much together, Fullerton and you; till somehow you had laughed yourself forever out of the solemn crowd for whom so many things are "all right in theory, but—". And that is already something.

"What can our criterion of reasoning be when we leave the sphere of the immediately palpable?" No one more ready than Fullerton to leave this sphere with you, so you would take reason for guide. The "plain argument" records one of these excursions, and would you know (you later men who have fallen into the hands of less lovable lovers of wisdom)—would you know the outcome?

"I have tried to make clear that the argument for God [so Fullerton writes in conclusion] is simply the natural argument for a mind revealed in the system of things.

"Throughout I have insisted upon keeping in mind the analogy between the argument for God and the reasoning which convinces us of the existence of minds in other men. In the light of this analogy, objections to the argument from the reign of natural law, from the eternity of the world, and from the doctrine of evolution have been seen to be quite aside from the point at issue.

"And it will be well to remember that we may very possibly get help in any new difficulties which may meet us in reflecting upon the idea of God, if we will adhere closely to this thought.

"There is, so far as I can see, only one way in which the student of natural science may refute our argument for God. If he ever succeeds in proving that nature is irrational, and that things do not reveal mind, he will have answered the argument. Whatever else he may succeed in proving, unless he establish this, he leaves the argument untouched." (Collected.)

Fullerton, you see, was not always laughing. Was he ever? I wonder. Or was he, out of a heart knowing its own bitterness, dispensing a lightness it was his to give rather than keep? I wonder. But as though it were play we learned to think: and to think in the end, of—what? Of such things as I have said, and to think of these things with that highest reverence: the reverence of enquiring reason.

Of Fullerton's later years (after 1904) but faint echoes have reached me. This one followed his course at Columbia, that one found him at home in Munich, another heard him lecture at Vienna. All bring impressions: impressions of a brilliant mind, of a personality, of charm, of a humanity at once kind and—baffling. Too vague all this to set down beside our clearer memories. For others, Fullerton was always a distinguished man; with us, he was a tradition.

And now I would willingly hope these notes revealing the impressions left long ago by the personality of a thinker, may not have spent all they have to offer, in paying tribute of old pupil and old friend to a cherished memory. He whom they recall belongs not only to his classes but through his writings to the public. Would it not be strange if the workman had so excluded his personality from the work that no new insight into his private being could help in the interpretation of his public utterance?

Yet what I would suggest in the way of such "help" must have a strangeness of its own. It is that Fullerton, more than any other I know of, tried to keep what was deepest in himself out of his expression: he tried to keep to himself the gropings of his soul.

There is, I venture to say, not a single fellow-alumnus having shared with me the "hours" just recalled who will not have heard the same "fault-found" with Fullerton, the teacher: "Never will he let us know the final answer, never trust us with *the end of his thought.*" There were those from whom this complaint came with a certain depth of disappointment; there were others for whom it was no more than an amused appreciation of an outwitting cleverness; there were a few perhaps who saw this "fault" as a shining merit. "Not to tell *what he* thinks, but *how one* thinks is the thinker's use to us,"

these would say.   No doubt Fullerton would
have accepted this last account of his motives;
no doubt he would have offered himself no
other.

If I have come to think there may have
been a deeper reason for this reserve, perhaps
another reminiscence will hint the way to it
—a memory, this time, of Harvard days.
There, Dean Everett (of Divinity) was
known for one of those sweet-souled gentlemen whose humor, too abundant to be re-
pressed, was yet too cautiously kind to risk
itself on any object but its author.   When
then this teacher (who like Fullerton was
preacher, too) would enforce his precepts on
the last touch to be given a homily, he would
sometimes offer himself as sound example.
"And when, gentlemen [so his words were
repeated to me], having of a Saturday carefully reread my Sunday discourse I could
assure myself, here was nothing could hurt
any one—then I knew there was no more
to be done."

The reader will be good enough to recall
the "plain argument" as in a previous paragraph I brought it back to those who had

shared undergraduate days with me. In those days, as ever after, Fullerton was fond of letting the convinced tones of Berkeley plead the "analogy" on which all depended:

"It is plain we do not see a *man*—if by *man* is meant that which moves, perceives, and thinks as we do—but only such a certain collection of ideas as directs us to think there is a distinct principle of thought and motion, like to ourselves, accompanying and represented by it. And after the same manner we see God; all the difference is that, whereas some one finite and narrow assemblage of ideas denotes a particular human mind, whithersoever we direct our view, we do at all times and in all places perceive manifest tokens of Divinity—everything we see, hear, feel or anywise perceive by sense, being a sign or effect of the power of God; as in our perception of those very motions which are produced by men" (*Pr.* 148).

With no more than this the "plain argument" of our undergraduate day closed. But it is not to be supposed that at this point Fullerton's critical mind stopped thinking; no more *then* than a few years later when (in the *System of Metaphysics*, 1904) immediately following this passage from Berkeley comes the comment:

"But it must be admitted that the inference that there is a God rests upon an analogy much more remote than that on which we rest the inference that the minds of other men exist" (601).

Nor can I conceive Fullerton himself to have derived any real comfort from a later reflection of this same work: after all, the inference to the Divine Mind may not appear so "much more remote" than the inference to fellow-minds, if we do but reflect *how little we have a right to know of these fellow-minds*.

"All of which means that we may make inferences touching minds without being able as yet to bring such inferences under the head of truths scientifically proved. The inference to the existence of God seems to be of the same nature. To many men—and not necessarily to the ignorant and the unreflective—the conviction that a Divine Mind is revealed in the world seems an irresistible one.

"[But] it is scarcely too much to say that if his experience of the world and the facts of his own life do not at least incline a man to recognize the analogy upon which the inference of God's existence rests, it is not likely that he will be convinced by reading.

"With those who do admit the analogy, I am glad to enroll myself.

"But [Fullerton characteristically adds] I think it important to recognize that the analogy is a remote one. One gains nothing by pretending to more information than one really has, or by confusing Faith with established knowledge" (604, 5).

What shall we say? is this argument one that can address itself only *ad fidem intellectum quaerentem?* And in the "Faith" of the last line, has it found such a faith? At least it will have caught this faith in no unwary mood; it is Fullerton himself who but a few pages before had issued the warning:

"The *fides quaerens intellectum,* the faith that already has its conclusion, and is casting about for premises, is always in some danger of accepting premises uncritically" (573).

One gains nothing by pretending to more

information than one really has!   And yet,
what *of* this "Faith" that will not "pretend"
to reason?

We sometimes feel das unglücklichen, das
insichentzweiten Bewusstsein of history to
have had moments of a worried repose-of-
exhaustion.   Mr. Fausset (in his recent *Study
in Discord*) recalls John Donne's animadver-
sion on this motive of Faith:

"I begin to think that as litigious men tired
with suits admit any arbitrament, and princes
travailed with long and wasteful war descend
to such conditions of peace as they are soon
after ashamed to have enhanced, so philosophers, and so all sects of Christians, after
long disputations and controversies, have allowed many things for dogmatical truths
which are not worthy of that dignity; and
so, many doctrines have grown into the ordinary diet and food of our spirits, . . . which
were admitted but as physic in that present
distemper, or accepted in a lazy weariness,
when men, so they might have something
to rely upon, and to excuse themselves from
a more fanciful inquisition, never examined
what that was" (140).

But such moods, while they do befall all philosophers, and the religious consciousness of whatever sympathies, can endure only in the collective, the institutional mind of "sects" and communions. Donne himself was witness to the impermanency of the rest that rests on strife-weariness alone. The individual mind quickly recovers its critical spirit, and the more its faith is dear to it the more it torments itself anew. It can not long "excuse itself from a more fanciful inquisition"; it must sooner or later examine *what that physic was,* or rather what "present distemper" cried for physic at all.

There are those who would find Fullerton, whatever his distemper had been, finally to have exorcized it with a word,—a word coming more and more frequently to his lips as his work grew in years. That word is "loyalty." "Traditions" come to voice for him no mere irrationalities of simpler times, but the best experience of the ages. Traditions of patriotism, of respect for law—all that "established order of things"—become endowed for him with a certain sacredness by virtue of all the human travail gone into their

making. A religion that had at one time
been content with a "plain argument," had
then grown critical of this "reasoning," had
for a moment appealed to a Faith outstrip-
ping reason, came in the end to advocate
faith in tradition. Why? Because *this* faith
could at least be argued? The original, the
ever-returning demand for argued and reasoned faith doubtless persisted; but who re-
calling the critical intellect of Fullerton can
suppose his spirit to have fed *itself* on such
(aggressively sane but) unexamined proprie-
ties of thought as the *Handbook of Ethical
Theory* (1922) offers to its undergraduate
audience? . . .

"A woman [we find it there written] may
regret that her infant has red hair. She will
not, on that account, as a rule, exchange him
surreptitiously for another. Men do not
commonly repudiate their fathers because
they are not rich or are growing old. A good
citizen may regret that his country has seen
fit to enter into a given war, but he will not,
therefore, give aid or comfort to the enemy.

"He who is capable of lightly repudiating
his religion resembles the man who is capable

of discarding his wife, when he sees the first gray hair. Those who do such things are apt to be men who fill their whole field of vision with their rights, and can find no place there for their duties. Nor should it be overlooked that the man who is capable of lightly discarding his wife is the man as capable of supplying her place with a worse. Even so, he who easily throws off his religion is usually the man who easily replaces it with some superstition, scientific or merely whimsical, at which other men wonder" (352 f.).

"I maintain that tradition and loyalty have their claims. They are not the only claims that can be made, but they are worthy of serious consideration. Man is man, whether he is dealing with things secular or things religious" (360)

It is astonishing how as I read these lines there comes back to me the old feeling of the "end of the hour,"—of an hour that ended thirty-odd years ago. We had no words for it then—just a vague sense of something restless abroad; while a grave kindly voice seemed to laugh our uneasiness away. But if now, with the experience of a life-time behind him, one who recalled those "ends of the hour" were to seek words for his remembered mood, perhaps he would find some such as these: " 'All is questionable; but let us trust all is well with the world—and beyond.' This is what Fullerton would have *us* take abroad with us. But what does that questioning mind of his carry back to its own solitudes?"

There are times when hearing my colleagues complain of Fullerton's "inconclusiveness" I have seemed to catch the old student-spirit surviving in a mature word. And then I have wondered whether throughout the whole of this life there had not run a single unavowed motive of reticence. Was he not essentially a pastor of the flock? Had he not sat so long at the feet of the Preacher that, like the gentle soul of my Harvard memory, he must always run a last anxious eye over his homily to make sure "there was nothing there could hurt"? And what if his fully expressed and most critical thought refused him this assurance? Then the "last word" must be deleted, must it not?

Where did this word-that-hurt, forbidden its proper place, find ultimate lodgment?   In what martyrdoms may not a repression of the critical spirit end?